# DOSAGE CALCULATIONS IN SI UNITS

**MAUREEN OSIS, R.N., M.N.**

The C. V. Mosby Company Ltd.
Toronto

A TRADITION OF PUBLISHING EXCELLENCE

Manuscript editor:  B.C. Decker Inc.
Design:  B.C. Decker Inc.
Production:  B.C. Decker Inc.
Cover Design:  Joe Cosentino

Printed in Canada, by Bryant Press.
International Standard Book Number 0–8016–3863–1
The C.V. Mosby Company Ltd.

 3 4 5 BP 90 89

Canadian Cataloguing in Publication Data

   Osis, M. (Maureen)
     **Dosage Calculations in SI Units**

   Bibliography: p.
   ISBN 0–8016–3863–1

   1. Drugs—Dosage.  2. Pharmaceutical arithmetic.  I. Title.

   RS57.085 1986    615′.14    C86–090150–5

# PREFACE

In 1859 Florence Nightingale commented on a method of dosage calculation. She wrote:

> "I have known several of our real old-fashioned "sisters", who could, as accurately as a measuring glass, measure out all their patients' wine and medicine by the eye, and never be wrong. I do not recommend this, one must be very sure of one's self to do it."

Florence Nightingale
Notes on Nursing, 1859

Today in many clinical settings dosage calculations cannot be "measured by eye". One requires knowledge of systems of measurement, arithmetic skills, conceptual skills of stating a calculation problem, as well as being "very sure of one's self." This book will help you gain all of these.

The purpose of this book is to give the reader the opportunity to assess and master the skills required to calculate dosages accurately in many clinical settings. It provides a comprehensive review of basic arithmetic, calculation concepts, and relies on SI units throughout. It is designed according to the principles of individualized learning with competence as its goal.

*Dosage Calculations in SI Units* is written by a nurse and designed primarily for nursing students, nursing refresher students, and practicing nurses who recognize the need to upgrade their skills. It will interest individuals who are unfamiliar with SI units as well as those who are changing their practice setting. Other health professionals who are involved in dosage calculations will also find the material useful.

This book can be used independently or as an adjunct to classroom lectures and clinical conferences. Within each module examples and exercises proceed from simple to more complex concepts. The presentation is based on a hierarchical ordering of concepts; thus, Module 10 requires more complex skills than does Module 8. Each module provides a pre-test for assessment of skills, presentation of the concepts with relevant examples, exercises to ensure mastery of the concepts and skills, and a post-test to evaluate competence. The book includes answers to all pre-tests, exercises, and post-tests, providing immediate feedback and encouraging self-evaluation.

There are several distinguishing features of this book. The first is its reliance on the International System of Units, the official system of measurement in Canada. It differs slightly from the metric and is called "SI," from the French, le Système International d'Unités. The second is its minimal use of rules and formula and its emphasis on mastering calculation skills through alternative approaches. Additionally, the reader will note that a module on the preparation of solutions is not included, e.g., preparing a dilute solution from a concentrated stock solution. In contrast to the many books on math for nurses, that topic is intentionally omitted for several reasons.

The preparation, i.e., the dispensing of medications is clearly the pharmacist's legal and professional responsibility. If a dilute solution must be prepared, pharmacy should provide instructions for that preparation, in the same manner as pharmaceutical companies do on vials of powdered drugs requiring reconstitution. A survey of practicing hospital and community health nurses, each with more than ten years' experience, revealed that none considered the mixing of solutions to be a clinical nursing responsibility. The book does include the calculation of intravenous flow rates, which is a relevant and commonly required clinical skill.

The book's design facilitates self-paced learning. This is appropriate in view of the varied baseline arithmetic skills of the intended audience. Some individuals will complete all modules in two to three hours with little difficulty. Others may require 14 hours or more and will have to review some exercises and tests. The difference is a quantitative not a qualitative one. In both instances, ultimately, the individual will master the concepts.

A Computer Assisted Instruction Software program has been developed for use in conjunction with the book. It will make teaching and learning easier and can save you valuable class time. For more information concerning the software please contact your Mosby Marketing Representative or call 1–800–268–4178.

No book results from individual effort alone. There are many people I wish to acknowledge for their contribution to this project. I thank the reviewers Barb Carruthers, Humber College, Karen Wall, Red River Community College, Carrol Morris, Wascana Institute, Jennifer Cooke, George Brown Community College, for their very critical and helpful reviews of the manuscript. I thank Steve Long, B.Sc.Phm., Director of Pharmacy, Rockyview Hospital, for his assistance with the modules involving examples of medication orders. To the many nursing students, refresher nurses, and colleagues who tested and evaluated the manuscript, I express my gratitude for their invaluable contributions. I thank Robert Alongi for the illustrations. In particular I thank my family: Andrew for his kindness and humor, Lara for her creativity and joy, Sean for his enthusiasm and spirit, and Imants for his support and wisdom.

Maureen Osis, R.N., M.N.

# Contents

# How to use This Book

This workbook consists of ten modules. Each module has a pre-test—a learning package explaining the specific concepts, along with exercises to test your understanding—and a post-test. It is recommended, but not mandatory, that you proceed through the modules in sequence:

1. Begin with Module 1; write the pre-test to assess your skills in the module.

2. Correct the pre-test by using the answer guide at the end of the text.

3. If you achieve 100 percent in the pre-test, you may wish to omit the module learning package and proceed to the pre-test of the next module.

4. If you don't achieve 100 percent in the pre-test, read the module learning package and complete the exercises, concentrating on your weak areas as diagnosed by your pre-test score.

5. Correct the exercises by using the answers at the end of the module.

6. Write the post-test at the end of the module *without* referring to the module learning package or to any other resources, and without the aid of a calculator.

7. Correct the post-test using the answer guide at the end of the text.

8. Then if you achieve 100 percent, proceed to the next module.

9. If you don't achieve 100 percent in the post-test, analyze your problems. For example, are your errors related to one skill, such as division of fractions, or are you weak in several skills? Review the appropriate sections of the module's learning package until you improve your skills. You may wish to consult additional references, which are listed in the bibliography.

10. Rewrite the post-test.

**Note:** you are expected to achieve 100 percent because of the importance of accuracy when calculating drug dosages. You may be tempted to proceed if your test scores are "close" to the mark. However, you are encouraged to diagnose your errors carefully and master the arithmetic or calculation concept before you proceed. Further, you are instructed to do the calculations without the aid of a calculator. These instruments, while quick and accurate, have their limitations; e.g., dead batteries.

> **In this workbook some common drugs are used as examples. The generic name is given, with a Canadian brand name in brackets; such as, digoxin (Lanoxin).**
>
> **In these examples every effort has been made to refer to accurate and acceptable dosage schedules. The reader, however, is advised to refer to recent drug information before administering any drug.**

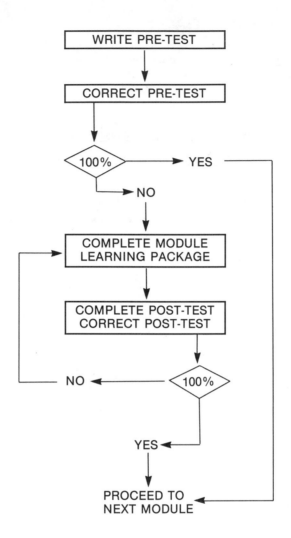

# Module 1: Arithmetic

## PRE-TEST

## Instructions

1. Write the pre-test without referring to any resources and without the aid of a calculator.

2. Correct the pre-test using the answer guide.

3. If your score is 100 percent, proceed to the next module.

4. If you don't achieve 100 percent accuracy, read the learning package in this module and complete the exercises, concentrating on your weak areas as diagnosed by your pre-test score.

## Addition of whole numbers:

| | | | | |
|---|---|---|---|---|
| 1. | 546<br>+ 677 | | 2. | 1 972<br>+ 545 |
| 3. | 729<br>+ 85 | | 4. | 139<br>+ 455 |
| 5. | 378<br>+ 521 | | 6. | 402<br>+ 99 |

## Subtraction of whole numbers:

| | | | | |
|---|---|---|---|---|
| 7. | 831<br>− 356 | | 8. | 1 897<br>− 543 |
| 9. | 396<br>− 85 | | 10. | 452<br>− 399 |
| 11. | 894<br>− 105 | | 12. | 401<br>− 299 |

## Multiplication of whole numbers:

13.     326
        × 8

14.     320
        × 17

15.     876
        × 59

16.     645
        × 13

17.     3 789
        × 235

18.     1 094
        × 2 001

## Division of whole numbers:

19.    7 )126

20.    250 )500

21.    11 )55

22.    12 )96

23.    25 )125

24.  326 )2 608

## Word problems:

25. The first hockey team had ten men on the ice, and six were given penalties for fighting. The second team had seven men on the ice, and all were given penalties for fighting. How many players were given penalties?
Answer: _____

26. The Canadian junior hockey team beat the West German club by a score of eight to two. How many more goals did the Canadians score than the West German players?
Answer: _____

27. There are ten women in the class, and there are twice as many men as women. How many people are in the class?
Answer: _____

28. There are forty-two patients on the ward and six nurses. Each nurse will care for how many patients?
Answer: _____

29. You return your overdue books to the library. The fine is one dollar a day. Three books are two days overdue, and two books are one week overdue. What is your total fine?
Answer: _____

30. A friend agrees to share evenly the library fine with you (question 29). How much will each of you pay?
Answer: _____

YOUR SCORE: _____ %

100%        YES—proceed to the next module
            NO—complete this module

---

**Note:** if you had any errors on the pre-test, analyze your areas of weakness here.

## Learning Package

> **Objective 1**
>
> **To demonstrate 100 percent accuracy in the arithmetic skills of addition, subtraction, multiplication, and division of whole numbers**

Because the rules for addition, subtraction, multiplication and division of whole numbers are very basic, they are not presented in this workbook. However, an example demonstrating each skill is included as a "memory refresher." If you aren't familiar with these skills, you should refer to a basic arithmetic textbook or the reference by Miller (1981) listed in the bibliography.
Additional exercises are provided for those who didn't achieve 100 percent in the pre-test.

## Addition of Whole Numbers

> Example:
>
> $$\begin{array}{r} \overset{1\ 1}{7\!\!\!/12} \\ +\ \ 89 \\ \hline 801 \end{array}$$

Remember to carry the tens, hundreds to the next column!

## Exercise 1.1

Complete the following exercise for practice. Do not use a calculator. Correct using the answer guide.

| | | | | | |
|---|---|---|---|---|---|
| 1. | 1 259<br>+ 368 | 2. | 106 789<br>+ 56 811 | 3. | 3 982<br>+ 4 902 |
| 4. | 10 094<br>+ 9 907 | 5. | 6 062<br>+ 5 903 | 6. | 309 485<br>+ 598 793 |

**Note:** the Metric Commission of Canada states that spaces are used to separate long numbers into three-digit blocks. With four-digit numbers the space is optional. This module encourages you to write numbers as illustrated in exercise 1.1. This rule also applies to decimal numbers. See Module 3.

## Subtraction of Whole Numbers

Example:

$$
\begin{array}{r}
{}^{6\,0} \\
\not{7}\not{1}2 \\
-\ 89 \\
\hline
623
\end{array}
$$

Remember to borrow from the tens or hundreds column!

## Exercise 1.2

Complete the following exercise for practice. Do not use a calculator. Correct using the answer guide.

1.    $\begin{array}{r} 588 \\ -\ 499 \\ \hline \end{array}$    2.    $\begin{array}{r} 600 \\ -\ 197 \\ \hline \end{array}$

3.    $\begin{array}{r} 458 \\ -\ 369 \\ \hline \end{array}$    4.    $\begin{array}{r} 125 \\ -\ 99 \\ \hline \end{array}$

5.    $\begin{array}{r} 301\ 984 \\ -\ 98\ 455 \\ \hline \end{array}$    6.    $\begin{array}{r} 98\ 273 \\ -\ 87\ 074 \\ \hline \end{array}$

## Multiplication of Whole Numbers

Example:

$$
\begin{array}{r}
{}^{1} \\
{}^{1\,1} \\
\not{7}\not{1}2 \\
\times\ 89 \\
\hline
6408 \\
5696\ \ \\
\hline
63368
\end{array}
$$

## Exercise 1.3

Complete the following exercise for practice. Do not use a calculator. Correct using the answer guide.

1.  $\begin{array}{r} 13 \\ \times\ 12 \\ \hline \end{array}$   2.  $\begin{array}{r} 984 \\ \times\ 359 \\ \hline \end{array}$

3.  $\begin{array}{r} 101 \\ \times\ 33 \\ \hline \end{array}$   4.  $\begin{array}{r} 78\ 903 \\ \times\ 45 \\ \hline \end{array}$

5.  $\begin{array}{r} 6\ 701 \\ \times\ 300 \\ \hline \end{array}$   6.  $\begin{array}{r} 405 \\ \times\ 63 \\ \hline \end{array}$

## Division of Whole Numbers

Example:

$$89\ \overline{)\begin{array}{l} \phantom{00}8 \\ 712 \\ 712 \\ \hline 000 \end{array}}$$

## Exercise 1.4

Complete for following exercise for practice. Do not use a calculator. Correct using the answer guide.

1.  $28\ \overline{)56}$   2.  $9\ \overline{)279}$

3.  $250\ \overline{)1\ 000}$   4.  $12\ \overline{)156}$

5.  $359\ \overline{)353\ 256}$   6.  $8\ \overline{)1\ 000}$

## Arithmetic of Whole Numbers: Additional Practice

### Exercise 1.5

Complete the following exercise for practice. Do not use a calculator. Correct using the answer guide.

1.  $225 \overline{)450}$

2.  $50 \overline{)1\ 100}$

3.  $56 \overline{)56}$

4.  $\begin{array}{r} 238 \\ \times\ 23 \\ \hline \end{array}$

5.  $\begin{array}{r} 909 \\ \times\ 10 \\ \hline \end{array}$

6.  $\begin{array}{r} 1\ 000 \\ \times\ 67 \\ \hline \end{array}$

7.  $\begin{array}{r} 302 \\ -\ 99 \\ \hline \end{array}$

8.  $\begin{array}{r} 27\ 985 \\ -\ 19\ 867 \\ \hline \end{array}$

9.  $\begin{array}{r} 30\ 301 \\ +\ 226 \\ \hline \end{array}$

10.  $\begin{array}{r} 101 \\ +\ 99 \\ \hline \end{array}$

## Arithmetic of Whole Numbers in Word Problems

Solving word problems using basic arithmetic skills is somewhat different from solving number problems, in that you must set up the mathematical equation. Due to the importance of reading a problem and setting it up when calculating dosages in the real world, the following problems are provided for practice. Have fun with these situations.

## Exercise 1.6

Complete the following exercise for practice. Do not use a calculator. Correct using the answer guide.

1. Today—the date isn't important—I went to the corner store—and that isn't important, either—and bought a drink for one dollar, a chocolate bar for two dollars and a six pack of doughnuts for three dollars and fifty cents. How much did I spend?
Answer: _____

2. The sports store is having a super ski sale. Skis that regularly cost three hundred and ninety-nine dollars now cost one hundred and thirty-seven. How much could you save on a pair of skis?
Answer: _____

3. This week the farmers' market is advertising apples at twenty-five cents each. How much will a dozen cost?
Answer: _____

4. Ten four-year-old children came to the birthday party. There were thirty grab bags, contents unknown. How many could each child have? (One might also ask, how many headaches did the parents have!)
Answer: _____

5. I had two dollars and a craving for licorice. Each stick cost ten cents, and I spent one dollar and sixty cents. How many sticks did I buy, and how much money did I have left?
Answer: _____

# POST-TEST

## Instructions

1. Write the post-test without referring to any reference materials and without the aid of a calculator.

2. Correct the post-test using the answer guide.

3. If your score is 100 percent, proceed to the next module.

4. If you don't achieve 100 percent, analyze your problem. Did you make mistakes in one skill, e.g., multiplication? Review that skill. If you made mistakes in more than one skill, e.g., addition and division, then consult addition reference materials (see bibliography) or seek a remedial course in arithmetic skills.

## Addition of whole numbers:

1.    $\begin{array}{r} 16\ 873 \\ +\ 9\ 834 \\ \hline \end{array}$    2.    $\begin{array}{r} 29\ 384 \\ +\ 29\ 847 \\ \hline \end{array}$

3.    $\begin{array}{r} 225 \\ +\ 298 \\ \hline \end{array}$    4.    $\begin{array}{r} 309\ 198 \\ +\ 93\ 820 \\ \hline \end{array}$

5.    $\begin{array}{r} 123 \\ +\ 678 \\ \hline \end{array}$    6.    $\begin{array}{r} 789 \\ +\ 345 \\ \hline \end{array}$

## Subtraction of whole numbers:

7.    $\begin{array}{r} 9\ 040 \\ -\ 3\ 909 \\ \hline \end{array}$    8.    $\begin{array}{r} 230 \\ -\ 199 \\ \hline \end{array}$

9.    $\begin{array}{r} 90 \\ -\ 27 \\ \hline \end{array}$    10.    $\begin{array}{r} 405 \\ -\ 176 \\ \hline \end{array}$

11.         989          12.        1 001
          − 798                    −  99

## Multiplication of whole numbers:

13.          23          14.          345
          × 89                     × 609


15.         102          16.          125
          × 303                     ×   8


17.       1 010          18.          423
          ×  10                     ×  11


## Division of whole numbers:

19.      9 )‾2‾7‾          20. 11 )‾1‾ ‾1‾1‾1‾


21.   33 )‾6‾ ‾6‾3‾3‾        22.  12 )‾1‾0‾8‾


23. 601 )‾2‾4‾ ‾0‾4‾0‾        24. 25 )‾1‾ ‾0‾0‾0‾


## Word problems:

25.  The hockey arena sold 14 300 season tickets and 500 single-game tickets. Of these, nine hundred and seventy-eight were sold to nurses. How many ''civilians'' were at that game?
Answer: _____

26. One box of chocolate bars contains twenty-five bars, at a cost of fifty cents each. What is the total cost of the box?
Answer: _____

27. Forty-five nursing students went to a nightclub to listen to a new comedian. Each table had nine chairs. How many tables did this group need?
Answer: _____

28. Admission to the nightclub is regularly four dollars and fifty cents. If more than one dozen in a group buy tickets, the cost is reduced by fifty cents each. If more than twenty buy tickets, the cost is further reduced by fifty cents. For each additional five individuals in the group, the cost is reduced by twenty-five cents. How much did these enterprising nursing students—in question 27—each pay to see this comedian?
Answer: _____

29. Your total library fine is five dollars and fifty cents. The fine per day is fifty cents. How many days overdue is your book?
Answer: _____

30. Designer jeans usually priced at one hundred forty-nine dollars and ninety cents have been reduced by nineteen dollars and seventy-five cents. What is the price for the jeans? (Would you want them at this price?)
Answer: _____

YOUR SCORE: _____ %

100%        YES—proceed to the next module
            NO—review this module

**Note:** if you had any errors on the post-test, analyze your areas of weakness here.

# Module 2: Fractions

## PRE-TEST

### Instructions

1. Write the pre-test without referring to any resources and without the aid of a calculator.
2. Express all fractions in their lowest terms.
3. Correct the pre-test using the answer guide.
4. If your score is 100 percent, proceed to the next module.
5. If you don't achieve 100 percent accuracy, read the learning package in this module and complete the exercises, concentrating on your weak areas, as diagnosed by your pre-test score.

### Addition of fractions:

1. $\frac{2}{5} + 3\frac{1}{4} =$

2. $\frac{1}{3} + \frac{7}{10} + \frac{1}{5} =$

3. $2 + \frac{3}{4} =$

4. $3\frac{1}{8} + 4\frac{1}{6} =$

### Subtraction of fractions:

5. $\frac{7}{8} - \frac{2}{9} =$

6. $1\frac{1}{4} - \frac{3}{5} =$

7. $3 - \frac{7}{16} =$

8. $9\frac{3}{8} - 6\frac{7}{16} =$

## Multiplication of fractions:

9.    $\frac{2}{3} \times \frac{3}{4} =$

10.    $3\frac{1}{4} \times 4\frac{1}{2} =$

11.    $16 \times \frac{3}{10} =$

12.    $3\frac{1}{2} \times 9 =$

## Division of fractions:

13.    $\frac{16}{27} \div \frac{2}{3} =$

14.    $1\frac{1}{2} \div \frac{1}{2} =$

15.    $76 \div \frac{3}{4} =$

16.    $\frac{9}{16} \div 3 =$

## Change these improper fractions to mixed numbers:

17.    $\frac{18}{5} =$

18.    $\frac{83}{11} =$

19.    $\frac{49}{6} =$

20.    $\frac{127}{34} =$

## Find the lowest common denominator for:

21.    $\frac{1}{2}$ and $\frac{1}{4}$

22.    $\frac{1}{5}$ and $\frac{1}{6}$

23. $\frac{5}{8}$ and $\frac{2}{5}$

24. $\frac{2}{3}$ and $\frac{7}{8}$

## Reduce these fractions to their lowest terms:

25. $\frac{21}{24}$ =

26. $\frac{18}{72}$ =

27. $\frac{6}{9}$ =

28. $\frac{15}{35}$ =

## Identify the following expressions as proper or improper fractions or mixed numbers:

29. $\frac{7}{15}$

30. $\frac{21}{11}$

31. $1\frac{7}{8}$

32. $\frac{1}{30}$

## Express each fraction as an equivalent fraction:

33. $\frac{1}{2} = \frac{?}{6}$

34. $\frac{3}{20} = \frac{9}{?}$

35. $\frac{7}{9} = \frac{?}{27}$

36. $\frac{7}{10} = \frac{49}{?}$

## Word problems:

37.  There are thirty-six students in the class. One-half achieved a B grade and another quarter achieved honors. The remaining students failed the exam. How many students failed the exam?
Answer: _____

38.  A pie was divided into eighths. One individual ate one piece; a second individual ate three pieces. How much of the pie is left?
Answer: _____

39.  In a survey of seventy-two people, $\frac{1}{6}$ preferred brand "x" and $\frac{7}{18}$ preferred brand "y". The remainder chose brand "z". How many chose brand "z"?
Answer: _____

40.  In an election, $\frac{1}{4}$ of the voters liked candidate Smith; $\frac{5}{8}$ disliked the candidate. How many voters were undecided?
Answer: _____

YOUR SCORE: _____ %

100%      YES—proceed to the next module
          NO—complete this module

**Note:** if you had any errors on this pre-test, analyze your areas of weakness here.

# Learning Package

### Objective 2

**To demonstrate 100 percent accuracy in the arithmetic skills of addition, subtraction, multiplication, and division of mixed numbers and fractions**

## Definitions

The word *fraction* is from the Latin fractus, meaning "broken." A fraction is a number that represents a part of a whole unit. Figure 2.1 illustrates the concept of fractions.

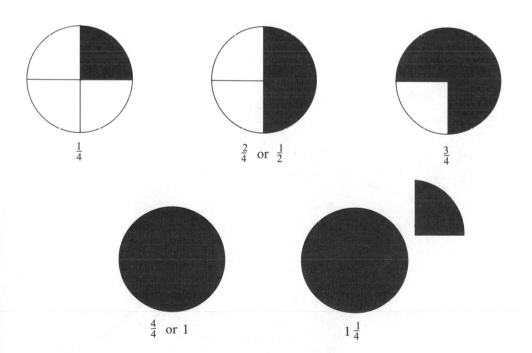

$\frac{1}{4}$

$\frac{2}{4}$ or $\frac{1}{2}$

$\frac{3}{4}$

$\frac{4}{4}$ or 1

$1\frac{1}{4}$

**Figure 2.1**   Fractions

The *numerator* is the top value.
The *denominator* is the bottom value.

> Example: $\frac{3}{4}$
>
> The numerator is 3
> The denominator is 4

## Types of Fractions

*Proper:* the numerator is less in value than the denominator:

> Example: $\frac{1}{3}$

*Improper fraction:* the numerator is greater in value than the denominator. It may be changed to a *mixed number* or a *whole number*.

> Example: $\frac{4}{3}$

*Mixed number:* contains a whole number and a fraction.

> Example: $1\frac{1}{3}$

*Whole number:*

> Example: $\frac{8}{4}$
>
> $\frac{8}{4} = 2$

*Equivalent fractions:* have the same value but are expressed in different forms. A fraction can have both terms—numerator and denominator—multiplied by the same number without changing its value. Likewise, both terms of a fraction can be divided by the same number without changing its value. This is an important principle in the arithmetic of fractions.

Example: $\frac{1}{2} = \frac{2}{4}$

$1 \times 2 = 2$
$2 \times 2 = 4$

Example: $\frac{4}{8} = \frac{1}{2}$

$4 \div 4 = 1$
$8 \div 4 = 2$

*Lowest term:* refers to a fraction in which the numerator and denominator have the lowest possible value. This is accomplished by dividing the denominator and the numerator by the same number.

Example: $\frac{1}{2}$ is in its lowest term.

$\frac{2}{4}$ is not expressed in its lowest term.

It can be reduced by:

1. Dividing both the numerator and the denominator by the same number; in this example, by 2.
2. Placing the new value of the numerator over the new value of the denominator

$$\frac{2}{4} = \frac{?}{?}$$

1. $2 \div 2 = 1$
   $4 \div 2 = 2$

2. Equivalent fraction in lowest term is $\frac{1}{2}$

## Exercise 2.1

Complete the following exercise for practice. Correct using the answer guide.
Identify the following as proper fractions, improper fractions, or mixed numbers:

1. $\frac{2}{3}$

2. $\frac{6}{7}$

3. $1\frac{1}{3}$

4. $\frac{9}{7}$

5. $\frac{1}{17}$

6. $3\frac{1}{10}$

Reduce to the lowest term:

7. $\frac{5}{15} =$

8. $\frac{4}{8} =$

9. $\frac{100}{200} =$

10. $\frac{20}{32} =$

Reduce to the lowest term if fraction can be reduced:

11. $\frac{45}{92} =$

12. $\frac{36}{72} =$

13. $\frac{27}{55} =$

14. $\frac{2}{15} =$

Which of the following expressions are equivalent fractions?

15. $\frac{3}{8} = \frac{15}{30}$    Yes or No

16. $\frac{7}{25} = \frac{14}{50}$    Yes or No

17. $\frac{21}{30} = \frac{126}{180}$    Yes or No

18. $\frac{5}{7} = \frac{25}{35}$    Yes or No

Express each fraction in higher terms, as indicated:

19. $\frac{3}{7} = \frac{?}{21}$

20. $\frac{4}{5} = \frac{?}{20}$

21. $\frac{2}{3} = \frac{10}{?}$

22. $\frac{1}{5} = \frac{6}{?}$

## Changing Improper Fractions and Mixed Numbers

An improper fraction can be changed to a mixed number by dividing the numerator by the
denominator.

$$\boxed{\begin{array}{l} \text{Example: } \frac{4}{3} = 1\frac{1}{3} \\ \quad 4 \div 3 = 1\frac{1}{3} \end{array}}$$

Similarly, a mixed number may be changed to an improper fraction by:

1. multiplying the whole number by the denominator.
2. adding the numerator to the product.
3. placing the sum over the denominator.

Example:  $5\frac{1}{3} = \frac{16}{3}$

whole number: 5
denominator: 3
1. product: $5\times3=15$
2. add numerator: $15+1=16$
3. place over denominator: $\frac{16}{3}$

## Exercise 2.2

Complete the following exercise for practice. Correct using the answer guide.
Change to improper fractions:

1.  $6\frac{1}{8}$  —

2.  $5\frac{1}{2} =$

3.  $3\frac{2}{4} =$

4.  $7\frac{9}{10}$  —

5.  $12\frac{2}{3} =$

Change to mixed or whole numbers:

6.  $\frac{39}{8} =$

7.  $\frac{11}{4} =$

8.  $\frac{15}{5} =$

9.  $\frac{10}{3} =$

10.  $\frac{125}{12} =$

## Arithmetic of Fractions

### Adding Fractions

To add fractions with the same denominator:
1. Add the numerators.
2. Place the sum over the denominator.
3. Reduce to lowest term if necessary.

Example:  $\frac{1}{5} + \frac{2}{5}$
1.  $1+2=3$
2.  $\frac{3}{5}$

To add fractions with unlike denominators:

1. Find the common denominator. This is the smallest whole number that the denominators of two or more fractions will divide into evenly.
2. Convert each fraction to an equivalent fraction using the common denominator.
3. Add numerators and place the sum over the common denominator.
4. Reduce the answer to the lowest term.

---

Example: $\frac{1}{2} + \frac{2}{3} = ?$

1. The common denominator is 6; that is, both 2 and 3 divide evenly into this number.
2. Convert: $\frac{1}{2} = \frac{?}{6}$

   2 into 6 = 3, and 3 × 1 = 3; therefore $\frac{1}{2} = \frac{3}{6}$

   Convert: $\frac{2}{3} = \frac{?}{6}$

   3 into 6 = 2, and 2 × 2 = 4; therefore $\frac{2}{3} = \frac{4}{6}$
3. Add: $\frac{3+4}{6} = \frac{7}{6}$
4. Reduce: $\frac{7}{6} = 1\frac{1}{6}$

---

## Exercise 2.3

Complete the following exercise for practice. Reduce all fractions to lowest term. Correct using the answer guide.

1. $\frac{2}{3} + \frac{6}{7} =$     2. $\frac{1}{3} + \frac{3}{10} =$

3. $\frac{5}{6} + \frac{7}{8} =$     4. $\frac{21}{32} + \frac{5}{16} =$

5. $\frac{3}{4} + \frac{7}{8} =$     6. $\frac{3}{7} + \frac{1}{2} =$

7. $\frac{1}{5} + \frac{5}{6} =$     8. $\frac{2}{3} + \frac{1}{9} =$

9. $\frac{3}{4} + \frac{1}{5} =$     10. $\frac{9}{16} + \frac{3}{8} =$

## *Subtracting Fractions*

To subtract fractions that have the same denominator:

1. Subtract the numerators.
2. Place the answer over the denominator.
3. Reduce to lowest term if necessary.

These steps are illustrated in the following example.

> Example: $\frac{3}{4} - \frac{1}{4} = ?$
>
> 1. $3 - 1 = 2$
> 2. $\frac{2}{4}$
> 3. $\frac{2}{4} = \frac{1}{2}$

To subtract fractions with unlike denominators:

1. Find the common denominator.
2. Convert each fraction to an equivalent fraction using the common denominator.
3. Subtract the numerators and place the difference over the common denominator.
4. Reduce to the lowest term.

> Example: $\frac{5}{6} - \frac{3}{8} = ?$
>
> 1. The common denominator is 24
> 2. Convert: $\frac{5}{6} = \frac{?}{24}$
>
>    $24 \div 6$ is 4 and $4 \times 5 = 20$; therefore $\frac{5}{6} = \frac{20}{24}$
>
>    Convert: $\frac{3}{8} = \frac{?}{24}$
>
>    $24 \div 8 = 3$ and $3 \times 3 = 9$; therefore $\frac{3}{8} = \frac{9}{24}$
> 3. Subtract: $\frac{20 - 9}{24} = \frac{11}{24}$
> 4. Reduce: $\frac{11}{24}$ is expressed in the lowest term

# Exercise 2.4

Complete the following exercise for practice. Correct using the answer guide.

1. $\frac{3}{7} - \frac{1}{4} =$        2. $\frac{5}{6} - \frac{1}{5} =$

3. $\frac{2}{3} - \frac{1}{8} =$        4. $\frac{3}{4} - \frac{1}{5} =$

5. $\frac{2}{3} - \frac{4}{9} =$        6. $\frac{5}{8} - \frac{3}{5} =$

7. $\frac{1}{3} - \frac{1}{4} =$        8. $\frac{4}{5} - \frac{8}{15} =$

9. $\frac{5}{9} - \frac{7}{16} =$        10. $\frac{7}{8} - \frac{1}{3} =$

### Adding and Subtracting Mixed Numbers

To add or subtract mixed numbers, first convert the mixed number to an improper fraction, then follow the steps outlined above for addition and subtraction of fractions.

---

Example: $1\frac{1}{3} + \frac{3}{4} = ?$

Convert the mixed number:
$1\frac{1}{3}$ is $\frac{4}{3}$

Find the common denominator:
12 is evenly divided by both 3 and 4
Convert: $\frac{4}{3} = \frac{?}{12} = \frac{16}{12}$
Convert: $\frac{3}{4} = \frac{?}{12} = \frac{9}{12}$

Add numerators: $16 + 9 = 25$
Place sum over denominator: $\frac{25}{12}$
Reduce: $\frac{25}{12} = 2\frac{1}{12}$

---

Example: $2 - \frac{1}{2} = ?$

Convert the whole number to a fraction:
$2 = \frac{2}{1}$

Find the common denominator: 2
Convert: $\frac{2}{1} = \frac{?}{2} = \frac{4}{2}$
Convert: $\frac{1}{2} = \frac{1}{2}$

Subtract numerators: $4 - 1 = 3$
Place over the denominator: $\frac{3}{2}$
Reduce: $\frac{3}{2} = 1\frac{1}{2}$

---

## Exercise 2.5

Complete the following exercise for practice. Correct using the answer guide.

1. $1\frac{3}{7} + \frac{1}{2} =$      2. $2\frac{1}{5} + \frac{1}{5} =$

3. $5\frac{3}{4} + 1\frac{1}{3} =$      4. $2\frac{7}{8} + \frac{5}{6} =$

5. $3\frac{1}{9} + 1\frac{1}{9} =$      6. $1\frac{1}{3} - \frac{1}{4} =$

7. $2\frac{5}{9} - 1\frac{1}{3} =$      8. $4\frac{1}{5} - 2\frac{1}{10} =$

9. $3\frac{1}{2} - 1\frac{1}{4} =$      10. $1\frac{1}{7} - \frac{3}{4} =$

### Multiplication of Fractions

To multiply fractions:

1. Multiply the numerators.
2. Multiply the denominators.
3. Place the product of the numerator over the product of the denominators.
4. Reduce to lowest term.

> Example: $\frac{2}{3} \times \frac{5}{7} = ?$
> 1. Product of numerators: $2\times5=10$
> 2. Product of denominators: $3\times7=21$
> 3. $\frac{10}{21}$
> 4. $\frac{10}{21}$ is expressed in lowest term.

To multiply a fraction by a whole number:

1. Multiply only the numerator of the fraction by the whole number.
2. Place the product over the denominator.
3. Reduce to lowest terms if necessary, or express the whole number as a fraction and proceed as outlined above.

> Example: $5 \times \frac{3}{7} = ?$
> 1. $5 \times 3 = 15$
> 2. Place the product over the original denominator: $\frac{15}{7}$
> 3. Reduce: $\frac{15}{7} = 2\frac{1}{7}$
>
>    or
>
> 5 may be expressed as $\frac{5}{1}$, and $\frac{5}{1} \times \frac{3}{7} = \frac{15}{7} = 2\frac{1}{7}$

To multiply a fraction by a mixed number:

1. Change it to an improper fraction.
2. Multiply the numerators.
3. Multiply the denominators.
4. Place the products of the numerators over the products of the denominators.
5. Reduce to lowest term if necessary.

---

Example: $3\frac{1}{5} \times \frac{3}{4} = ?$

1. $3\frac{1}{5} = \frac{16}{5}$
2. $16 \times 3 = 48$
3. $5 \times 4 = 20$
4. $\frac{48}{20}$
5. Reduce: $\frac{48}{20} = 2\frac{2}{5}$

---

## Exercise 2.6

Complete the following exercise for practice. Correct using the answer guide.

1. $\frac{5}{7} \times \frac{2}{3} =$     2. $3 \times \frac{1}{3} =$

3. $\frac{1}{8} \times \frac{1}{2} =$     4. $\frac{7}{16} \times \frac{3}{7} =$

5. $\frac{3}{4} \times 100 =$     6. $\frac{5}{6} \times 7 =$

7. $\frac{2}{3} \times 4 =$     8. $1\frac{1}{4} \times 2\frac{1}{3} =$

9. $2 \times \frac{5}{8} =$     10. $10\frac{1}{4} \times \frac{1}{2} =$

## *Division of Fractions*

To divide fractions:

1. Invert the terms of the *divisor*. This is the number that is being divided into the *dividend*.
2. Then use multiplication.

---

Example: $\frac{1}{3} \div \frac{1}{2} = ?$

1. Invert the divisor: $\frac{1}{2} = \frac{2}{1}$
2. Multiply: $\frac{1}{3} \times \frac{2}{1} = \frac{2}{3}$

To divide a fraction by a whole number:

1. Express the whole number as a fraction.
2. Invert the divisor.
3. Use multiplication.
4. Reduce to lowest term if necessary.

> Example: $\frac{5}{6} \div 2 = ?$
>
> 1. 2 as a fraction is $\frac{2}{1}$
> 2. Invert: $\frac{2}{1}$ becomes $\frac{1}{2}$
> 3. Multiply: $\frac{5}{6} \times \frac{1}{2} = \frac{5}{12}$

To divide a fraction by a mixed number:

1. Change the mixed number to an improper fraction.
2. Invert the divisor.
3. Use multiplication.
4. Reduce to lowest term if necessary.

> Example: $\frac{3}{4} \div 1\frac{1}{8} = ?$
>
> 1. Convert to improper fraction:
>    $1\frac{1}{8} = \frac{9}{8}$
> 2. Invert the divisor: $\frac{9}{8} = \frac{8}{9}$
> 3. Multiply: $\frac{3}{4} \times \frac{8}{9} = \frac{24}{36}$
> 4. Reduce: $\frac{2}{3}$

## Exercise 2.7

Complete the following exercises for practice. Correct using the answer guide.

1. $\frac{5}{7} \div \frac{2}{3} =$     2.  $3 \div \frac{1}{3} =$

3. $2\frac{1}{8} \div \frac{1}{2} =$     4.  $\frac{7}{16} \div \frac{3}{7} =$

5. $\frac{3}{4} \div 100 =$     6.  $\frac{5}{8} \div \frac{1}{2} =$

7. $2\frac{3}{4} \div \frac{1}{8} =$     8.  $4 \div \frac{1}{3} =$

9. $1\frac{5}{6} \div 2\frac{3}{4} =$     10.  $100 \div \frac{2}{5} =$

## Arithmetic of Fractions in Word Problems

Using basic arithmetic skills, you can solve word problems requiring the addition, subtraction, multiplication, or division of fractions. In clinical settings, dosage calculations aren't written out like workbook problems. The following problems are provided for practice, in preparation for mastering the skills for calculating dosages of medications.

## Exercise 2.8

Complete the following exercise for practice. Correct using the answer guide.

1. Ingredients: $\frac{1}{8}$ cup of sugar, $\frac{1}{4}$ cup of water, $\frac{1}{5}$ cup of vegetables. The remainder is a secret sauce. What amount of the ingredients is known?
Answer: _____

2. Out of forty-five students in a class, $\frac{1}{9}$ fell asleep. How many stayed awake for the lecture?
Answer: _____

3. One of the students who fell asleep answered the following question:

$$\frac{4}{5} \times \frac{3}{2} = \frac{2}{4}$$

Is this answer correct?

Answer: _____

4. Another student answered the following question:

$$\frac{2}{6} \div \frac{4}{3} = \frac{2}{3}$$

Did the student answer correctly? (I won't ask whether you think this student stayed awake in class!)
Answer: _____

5. A bottle of liquid contains 30 ounces. Every day $\frac{1}{5}$ of the liquid is used. How much liquid remains on the third day?
Answer: _____

# POST-TEST

## Instructions

1. Write the post-test without referring to any reference materials and without the aid of a calculator.
2. Express all fractions in their lowest terms.
3. Correct the post-test using the answer guide.
4. If your score is 100 percent, proceed to the next module.
5. If you don't achieve 100 percent, analyze your problems and review the appropriate sections of the learning package in this module. Then rewrite the post-test or seek additional assistance from one of the references listed in the bibliography.

## Addition of fractions:

1.  $\frac{3}{4} + \frac{1}{7} =$    2.  $\frac{1}{8} + 1\frac{2}{5} =$

3.  $14 + \frac{7}{12} =$    4.  $\frac{5}{12} + \frac{3}{10} =$

## Subtraction of fractions:

5.  $\frac{8}{9} - \frac{5}{12} =$    6.  $2\frac{1}{2} - \frac{1}{6} =$

7.  $21 - \frac{15}{16} =$    8.  $\frac{7}{8} - \frac{2}{3} =$

## Multiplication of fractions:

9.  $\frac{2}{9} \times \frac{3}{7} =$    10.  $1\frac{1}{2} \times \frac{2}{5} =$

11.  $23 \times \frac{1}{3} =$    12.  $\frac{3}{4} \times 4 =$

## Division of fractions:

13.  $\frac{9}{16} \div \frac{3}{4} =$    14.  $3\frac{1}{4} \div \frac{1}{3} =$

15.  $\frac{5}{6} \div 2 =$    16.  $\frac{5}{9} \div \frac{7}{10} =$

## Change these improper fractions to mixed numbers:

17. $\frac{21}{5} =$        18. $\frac{38}{9} =$

19. $\frac{89}{7} =$        20. $\frac{203}{12} =$

## Find the lowest common denominator for:

21. $\frac{7}{9}$ and $\frac{3}{8}$        22. $\frac{15}{16}$ and $\frac{2}{3}$

23. $\frac{13}{18}$ and $\frac{23}{24}$        24. $\frac{5}{6}$ and $\frac{4}{7}$

## Reduce to the lowest terms:

25. $\frac{16}{36} =$        26. $\frac{25}{45} =$

27. $\frac{15}{18} =$        28. $\frac{12}{4} =$

29. Which of the following is a proper fraction? Circle your choice.

$$\frac{8}{9} \qquad \frac{4}{3} \qquad 1\frac{1}{4}$$

30. Which of the following is an improper fraction? Circle your choice.

$$\frac{7}{8} \qquad \frac{21}{30} \qquad \frac{14}{11}$$

31. Which of the following is a mixed number? Circle your choice.

$$1\frac{2}{3} \qquad \frac{7}{7} \qquad \frac{5}{9}$$

## Express the following fractions as equivalent fractions:

32. $\frac{5}{7} = \frac{35}{?}$        33. $\frac{14}{35} = \frac{28}{?}$

34. $\frac{5}{9} = \frac{?}{108}$        35. $\frac{3}{20} = \frac{?}{200}$

36. $\frac{8}{11} = \frac{32}{?}$

## Word problems:

37. Of thirty people, $\frac{8}{30}$ like skiing, $\frac{5}{30}$ like fishing, and the remaining don't like any sports. Expressed as a whole number, how many individuals would rather sit than participate?
Answer: _____

38. A bottle of aspirin contains 100 pills. If sixteen friends had simultaneous headaches and $\frac{1}{2}$ of them took 2 pills each, and $\frac{1}{4}$ took 1 pill each, how many aspirin would remain?
Answer: _____

39. If you attend a 2-hour lecture and spend $\frac{5}{6}$ of the time taking notes, how many minutes do you rest your hand?
Answer: _____

40. You have just completed the second of 10 modules. Express that as a fraction.
Answer: _____

YOUR SCORE: _____ %

100%        YES—proceed to the next module
                NO—review this module

---

**Note:** if you had any errors on the post-test, analyze your areas of weakness before reviewing the module.

# Module 3: Decimals

## PRE-TEST

## Instructions

1. Write the pre-test without referring to any resources and without the aid of a calculator.
2. Correct the pre-test using the answer guide.
3. If your score is 100 percent, proceed to the next module.
4. If you don't achieve 100 percent accuracy, read the learning package in this module and complete the exercises, concentrating on your weak areas as diagnosed by your pre-test score.

**Note:** be careful to write the decimal numbers correctly—according to the rules—and do *not* round off any numbers unless instructed to do so.

**For each of the following pairs, choose the correct way of writing decimals. Circle your choice:**

1.  .25 or 0.25          2.  1.0 or 1

3.  0.120 or 0.12

**Round off the following decimals to the nearest tenth:**

4.  3.43          5.  7.09

6.  1.239          7.  9.16

**Round off the following decimals to the nearest hundredth:**

8.  12.459          9.  6.096

10.  34.002          11.  4.909

**Addition of decimals:**

12.  $1.567 + 0.98 =$          13.  $123.5 + 2.534\ 2 =$

14.  $0.4 + 5.6 + 0.27 =$          15.  $2.1 + 0.53 + 1.102 =$

## Subtraction of decimals:

16.     $10 - 3.7 =$                     17.     $4.2 - 0.9 =$

18.     $5.6 - 1.08 =$                   19.     $0.125 - 0.075 =$

## Multiplication of decimals:

20.  $0.8 \times 10 =$                   21.     $0.8 \times 100 =$

22.  $0.8 \times 1\ 000 =$               23.     $0.1 \times 0.01 =$

## Division of decimals:

24.  $0.25 \div 0.5 =$                   25.     $100 \div 1.5 =$

26.  $0.667 \div 0.3 =$                  27.     $1.78 \div 0.04 =$

## Convert into decimals. Round off to the nearest tenth:

28.     $\frac{4}{5} =$                  29.     $\frac{1}{2} =$

30.     $\frac{1}{4} =$                  31.     $\frac{3}{4} =$

## Convert into fractions. Reduce to lowest terms:

32.     $0.6 =$                          33.     $0.57 =$

34.     $1.25 =$                         35.     $0.01 =$

## Arrange in size from smallest to largest:

36.     0.01            0.000 1          0.1            1.001            1.101

## Word problems:

37. John had $0.40 and Susan had twice as much money as John. In total, how much money did they have?
Answer: _____

38. A baseball glove costs $36.95. David has $48.65. How much will he have left after he buys the glove?
Answer: _____

39. A soccer team won the game and the coach bought pizzas. She ordered twelve pizzas and each cost $7.95. How much did she pay?
Answer: _____

40. Together, four girls earned $45.48. How much did each girl earn?
Answer: _____

YOUR SCORE: _____ %

100%    YES—proceed to the next module
NO—complete this module

---

**Note:** if you had any errors on the pre-test, analyze your areas of weakness here.

## Learning Package

---

**Objective 3**

**To demonstrate 100 percent accuracy in the arithmetic skills of addition, subtraction, multiplication, and division of decimals, and in converting decimals, percent, and fractions**

---

*Decimal numbers* express values that describe both whole units and portions of whole units. Decimal numbers include a decimal point and values to the right and left of the decimal. The numbers written to the left of the decimal point are whole numbers. The numbers written to the right of the decimal point are decimal fractions, that is fractions with denominators in multiples of ten.

Thus:

$$0.1 \; = \; \tfrac{1}{10} \; \text{or one-tenth}$$

$$0.01 \; = \; \tfrac{1}{100} \; \text{or one-hundredth}$$

$$0.001 = \; \tfrac{1}{1\,000} \; \text{or one-thousandth}$$

Figure 3.1 illustrates these concepts.

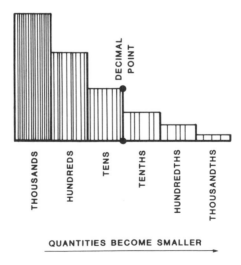

**Figure 3.1**   Decimal Numbers

> Example: In the number 6.125 there are:
>
> 6 units
>
> $\frac{1}{10}$ or one-tenth
>
> $\frac{2}{100}$ or two-hundreths
>
> $\frac{5}{1\,000}$ or five-thousandths

The size of decimal numbers can be compared by examining the values in each position to the right and left of the decimal point.

> Example: Which is larger  0.5 or 0.05?
>
> 0 ones    0.5        5 tenths
>
> 0 ones    0.05       0 tenths, 5 hundredths
>
> Therefore, 0.5 is larger than 0.05

## Rules for Writing Decimal Numbers

1. Always place a zero to the left of the decimal point when there are no whole numbers.

Example: 0.25 not .25

2. Never place a zero to the right of the decimal point.

Example: 1 not 1.0
1.2 not 1.20

These rules are extremely important when writing drug dosages. If a drug is ordered as 0.125 mg, the zero placed before the decimal highlights the point that might otherwise be missed. If 0.125 mg is misread as 125 mg, a fatal drug error could occur. Similarly, the zero placed after the decimal point is unnecessary. A drug order for 6 units is less likely to be misinterpreted than one written as 6.0 units. Missing the point could cause a tenfold error.

3. As with whole numbers, spaces are used to separate decimal numbers into three-digit blocks. (See Module 1)

Example: 1.000 1
1.078 35

### Rounding Off Decimal Numbers

Most calibrated devices used for medication administration are accurate only to the nearest tenth or hundredth. Module 7 illustrates these "tools of the trade"! Consequently, it is acceptable to round off dosage calculations.

To round off a decimal number:

1. Locate the digit furthest to the right of the decimal point.
2. If this digit is 5 or greater, add a value of 1 to the numeral to its immediate left.
3. If this digit is less than 5, do not increase the value of the numeral to its immediate left.
4. Continue this process one digit at a time moving right to left towards the decimal point.

---

Example: Round off 1.125 to the nearest hundredth.
1. The digit in the hundredth position is 2.
2. The digit to the right is 5.
3. Increase the value of the numeral in the hundredth place by 1.

Answer: 1.13

Round off 1.125 to the nearest tenth.
1. The digit in the tenth position is 1.
2. The digit to the right is 2.
3. Do not add value to the tenth.

Answer: 1.1

---

## Exercise 3.1

Complete the following exercise without referring to the previous text and without the aid of a calculator. Correct using the answer guide.

Some of the following decimal numbers violate the rules. Correct those that don't follow the rules.

1.  1.02            2.  1.70

3.  0.67            4.  .35

Round off these decimals to the nearest tenth:

5.  1.362           6.  1.94

7.  0.99            8.  1.07

Round off these decimals to the nearest hundredth:

9.  6.333 5         10.  2.090 9

11.  0.951          12.  7.666

13. Arrange the following in order from smallest to largest:

1.15            1.105            1.055            1.515

14. Arrange the following in order from largest to smallest:

5.06            50.6            0.506

# Arithmetic of Decimals

## *Addition and Subtraction of Decimals*

Decimal points must be lined up vertically, so that tenths are added to tenths, hundredths to hundredths, etc.

---

Addition

Example: $1.9+0.37+2.706$

$$
\begin{array}{r}
1.9 \\
0.37 \\
\underline{2.706} \\
4.976
\end{array}
$$

---

Subtraction

Example: $2.75-0.59$

$$
\begin{array}{r}
2.75 \\
\underline{-0.59} \\
2.16
\end{array}
$$

---

# Exercise 3.2

Complete the following exercise without referring to the previous text and without the aid of a calculator. Correct using the answer guide.

1. $3.51+2.03+0.9=$         2.   $10.1+3.27+1.003=$

3. $27.3-16.09=$           4.   $5.03-3.27 =$

5. $0.056+1.990\ 1=$        6.   $40\ 076.5-1.679\ 3=$

## *Multiplication of Decimals*

The multiplication of decimals follows the same rules as those for the multiplication of whole numbers. To determine the placement of the decimal point:

1. Count the number of digits to the right of the decimal point in each of the numbers being multiplied.

2. Add these numbers.
3. Place the decimal with this number of digits to the right.

---

Example: $2.162 \times 13.4 = ?$

1.  2.162: 3 digits to the right
2.  13.4: 1 digit to the right

The answer must have 4 digits to the right of the decimal point.

$$\begin{array}{r} 2.162 \\ \times\ 13.4 \\ \hline 8648 \\ 6486\phantom{0} \\ 2162\phantom{00} \\ \hline 289708 \end{array}$$

3.  Place decimal point with 4 digits to the right: 28.970 8

---

### Division of Decimals

To divide decimal numbers:

1. Write the problem as you would for the division of whole numbers.
2. Move the decimal place to the right in the divisor, so that it becomes a whole number. This is achieved by multiplying by 10, 100, or 1 000, etc.
3. Move the decimal point the same number of positions to the right in the dividend; that is, multiply both the divisor and the dividend by 10, 100, or 1 000, etc.

---

Example: $2.5\ \overline{)12.55} = ?$

Divisor is 2.5
Dividend is 12.55
Multiply both the divisor and the dividend by 10; that is, move the decimal point one place to the right in *both* numbers.

$$\begin{array}{r} 5.02 \\ 25\ \overline{)125.5} \\ \underline{125}\phantom{.5} \\ 0.5 \\ \underline{0.50} \\ .00 \end{array}$$

---

## Exercise 3.3

Complete the following exercise without referring to the previous text and without the aid of a calculator. Correct using the answer guide.

1.   $1.27 \times 3.2 =$                      2.   $2.73 \times 1.4 =$

3.   $10.078 \times 0.34 =$                   4.   $1.900\ 1 \times 30.6 =$

5.   $1.29 \div 0.3 =$                        6.   $17.588 \div 0.02 =$

7.   $0.25 \div 0.5 =$                        8.   $1\ 000.25 \div 0.001 =$

### Converting Fractions and Decimals

To convert a fraction to a decimal:
1. Divide the numerator by the denominator.

---
Example: $\frac{1}{2} = ?$

$1 : 2 = 0.5$
---

To convert a decimal to a fraction:
1. Determine the denominator as 10, 100, 1 000, etc. by the number of digits to the right of the decimal point.
2. Express as a fraction by placing the number over the selected denominator.
3. Reduce if necessary.

---
Example:
0.6 has 1 digit to the right
    = tenths or $\frac{6}{10}$
0.06 has 2 digits to the right
    = hundredths or $\frac{6}{100}$
0.006 has 3 digits to the right
    = thousandths or $\frac{6}{1\ 000}$
Convert: $0.06 = ?$
1. The denominator is 100
2. $\frac{6}{100}$
3. $\frac{3}{50}$
---

To convert a mixed number to a decimal:

1. Express the mixed number as an improper fraction.
2. Divide the numerator by the denominator.

---

Example: $1\frac{1}{4} = ?$

1. $1\frac{1}{4} = \frac{5}{4}$

2. $5 \div 4 = 1.25$

---

## Exercise 3.4

Complete the following exercise without referring to the previous text and without the aid of a calculator. Correct using the answer guide.

Convert the following decimals to proper or mixed fractions and express in the lowest terms:

| | | | |
|---|---|---|---|
| 1. | $0.125 =$ | 2. | $2.5 =$ |
| 3. | $0.6 =$ | 4. | $0.75 =$ |
| 5. | $1.75 =$ | | |

Convert the following fractions to decimals. Be certain to use a zero to the left of the decimal point where necessary.

| | | | |
|---|---|---|---|
| 6. | $\frac{3}{4} =$ | 7. | $\frac{1}{20} =$ |
| 8. | $3\frac{5}{6} =$ | 9. | $\frac{1}{3} =$ |
| 10. | $1\frac{1}{4} =$ | | |

### *Percent*

The relationship between percent and decimal numbers appears very confusing at first. However, the rules can be simplified.

*Percent* means "parts in a hundred." Our most frequent encounter with percentages is with relation to exam scores. For example, if your score is 90 percent, you answered 90 questions out of one hundred correctly. However, few exams have one hundred questions—thankfully! What does percent mean when there are only 30 rather than 100 parts?

Example: The exam has 30 questions, and you answered 12 questions correctly. Express your score as a percentage.

Express score as a fraction: $\frac{12}{30}$

Change fraction to a decimal:  0.4
Multiply decimal by 100:  40
Add the percent sign:  40%

Your score is 40%. This means that if the exam had 100 questions, you would have answered only 40 correctly. Hopefully this example isn't true for you!

To change a decimal number to a percent:

1. Multiply the decimal by 100.
2. Add the % sign.

Example:  0.67 = ?
1.  $0.67 \times 100 = 67$
2.  67%

To change a fraction to a percent:

1. Convert the fraction to a decimal number (previously explained in this module).
2. Multiply the decimal by 100.
3. Add the % sign.

Example:  $\frac{1}{5}$ = ?
1.  $\frac{1}{5} = 0.2$
2.  $0.2 \times 100 = 20$
3.  20%

To change a percent to a decimal:

1. Remove the percent sign.
2. Divide by 100.
3. Write the decimal number according to the rules.

Example:  40% = ?
1.  40
2.  $40 \div 100 = .4$
3.  0.4

## Exercise 3.5

Complete the following exercise without referring to the previous text and without the aid of a calculator. Correct using the answer guide.

Express these decimals as percents:

1.  1.5=

2.  0.37=

3.  0.17=

4.  0.94=

Express these fractions as percents:

5. $\frac{1}{15} =$                     6. $\frac{25}{30} =$

7. $\frac{8}{11} =$                      8. $\frac{79}{100} =$

Express these percents as decimals:

9.  77% =                              10.   1% =

11.  29% =                             12.  82% =

# POST-TEST

## Instructions

1. Write the post-test without referring to any reference materials and without the aid of a calculator.

2. Unless instructed otherwise, round off decimal numbers to the nearest hundredth.

3. Correct the post-test using the answer guide.

4. If your score is 100 percent, proceed to the next module.

5. If you don't achieve 100 percent accuracy, review the appropriate sections of the learning package in this module and rewrite the post-test, or seek additional assistance from one of the references listed in the bibliography.

## Addition of decimals:

1.    $1.347 + 2.8 =$

2.    $0.069 + 1.7 =$

3.    $1.21 + 0.05 =$

4.    $1.239 + 0.08 =$

## Subtraction of decimals:

5.    $3.52 - 1.19 =$

6.    $8.57 - 6.68 =$

7.    $18.09 - 16.9 =$

8.    $3.43 - 1.009\ 7 =$

## Multiplication of decimals:

9.    $5.06 \times 2.1 =$

10.    $10.1 \times 0.03 =$

11.    $2.5 \times 1.7 =$

12.    $1.01 \times 100 =$

## Division of decimals:

13.    $9 \div 0.05 =$        14.    $0.25 \div 2 =$

15.    $0.1 \div 0.05 =$        16.    $12.3 \div 4.1 =$

## Round off to the nearest tenth:

17.    4.15        18.    1.77

19.    1.26        20.    2.33

## Round off to the nearest hundredth:

21.    1.885        22.    1.973

23.    10.635        24.    0.359

## Convert these fractions to decimals:

25.    $\frac{2}{3} =$        26.    $1\frac{1}{4} =$

27.    $\frac{7}{8} =$        28.    $2\frac{1}{2} =$

## Convert these decimals to fractions. Reduce to lowest terms:

29.    $0.76 =$        30.    $1.3 =$

31.    $0.13 =$        32.    $0.05 =$

## Indicate which of the following correctly express the decimals according to the rules. Circle your choice:

33.    $\frac{1}{2} = .5$ or $0.5$        34.    1.2 or 1.20

35.    1.010 or 1.01

## Arrange in size from smallest to largest:

36.    10.01        1.901        10.1        1.991

37. James had $437.62 in his bank account. He earned $13.46 and deposited it in the bank. What is his current bank balance?
Answer: _____

38. Jodi wanted to withdraw $18.25 from her bank account to purchase a photo album. She had $405.02 in the account. What is her balance after the withdrawal?
Answer: _____

39. Dave bought twenty-eight eggs at $0.14 each. How much did he spend?
Answer: _____

40. For the fiscal year 1986–1987 a company's profits were $22 139.88. If there are forty-two employees, how much will each receive as a bonus?
Answer: _____

YOUR SCORE: _____ %

100%      YES—proceed to the next module
             NO—review this module

**Note:** if you had any errors on the post-test, analyze your areas of weakness here.

# Module 4: Ratio and Proportion

## PRE-TEST

## Instructions

1. Write the pre-test without referring to any resource materials and without the aid of a calculator.

2. Correct the pre-test using the answer guide.

3. If your score is 100 percent, proceed to the next module.

4. If you don't achieve 100 percent accuracy, read the learning package in this module and complete the exercises, concentrating on your weak areas as diagnosed by your pre-test score.

Solve for n:

1. $3:n=1:15$

2. $9:n=3:4$

3. $\frac{n}{100} = \frac{5}{20}$

4. $\frac{25}{1} = \frac{100}{n}$

5. $\frac{8}{n} = \frac{12}{6}$

6. $\frac{1}{50} = \frac{n}{150}$

Express the following ratios as fractions, decimals, and percents. Reduce fractions to lowest term.

| Ratio | Fraction | Decimal | Percent |
|-------|----------|---------|---------|
| 1:100 | 7. | 8. | 9. |
| 1:5 | 10. | 11. | 12. |
| 4:1 000 | 13. | 14. | 15. |

16. You buy seven oranges and five apples. What is the ratio of oranges to apples?
Answer: _____

17. There are forty patients and eight staff members. What is the ratio of patients to staff? Express as a ratio in lowest terms.
Answer: _____

18. Your score is eighty-five percent on a math exam. What is the ratio of correct to incorrect answers? Express as a ratio in lowest terms.
Answer: _____

19. Define the term *ratio*.

20. Define the term *proportion*.

YOUR SCORE: _____ %.

100%     YES—proceed to the next module
         NO—complete this module

**Note:** if you had any errors on the pre-test, analyze your areas of weakness here.

## Learning Package

### Objective 4
**To solve for an unknown value using ratio and proportion; to express ratios as fractions, decimals, and percents**

### Definitions

*Ratio*: describes a relationship that exists between two quantities. For example, a class of nursing students has 2 male and 148 female students. The ratio of males to females may be expressed as:

$$\text{a to b} \qquad \text{or} \qquad \text{a:b} \qquad \text{or} \qquad \frac{a}{b}$$

In this class the ratio of male to female is:

$$2 \text{ to } 148 \qquad \text{or} \qquad 2:148 \qquad \text{or} \qquad \frac{2}{148}$$

Expressed in the lowest term, this ratio is: $\frac{1}{74}$

That is, for every 74 female students, there is 1 male student. (What do you think of this ratio? Your answer is probably influenced by your sex.)

In this sample, the ratio of male students to the total class would be expressed as follows:

$$\text{male:total} \quad = \quad 2:150 \qquad \text{or} \qquad 1:75$$

It is very important to be certain you are choosing the correct numbers for the ratio equation.

**Note:** the fraction form, expressed in lowest terms, is used throughout this module for ease in stating mathematical equations.

Example: out of a basket of 200 apples, 57 are red and the remaining apples are green.
The ratio of red to green is 57:143
The ratio of red to total basket is 57:200

Ratios are used commonly in everyday situations. When you are jogging, swimming, or cycling, perhaps you chart your performance in kilometres per hour or metres per minute. Walking at five kilometres per hour will burn up almost three calories per minute. Five kilometres per hour and three calories per minute are ratios.

Ratio can also describe the strength of a solution. This is described in more detail in module 8.

Ratios are frequently used in drug calculations. The dosage strength of a medication can be expressed as a ratio.

> Example:
> 1 tablet contains 300 mg of
> drug. Ratio is 300 mg per tablet,
> or 300 to 1 or 300:1.

## Exercise 4.1

Complete the following exercise without referring to the previous text and without the aid of a calculator. Correct using the answer guide. Express all ratios as fractions in lowest terms.

You answered 18 questions correctly on an exam with 20 questions.

1. What is the ratio of incorrect to correct answers?
Answer: _____

2. What is the ratio of correct to total answers?
Answer: _____

3. The drug bottle label states, "Each tablet contains 325 units." Express the ratio of this drug in units per tablet.
Answer: _____

4. A vial of liquid medication states that each teaspoon contains 25 units. Express the ratio of units per teaspoon.
Answer: _____

5. In every hour of television programming that you watch, you also "enjoy" 12 minutes of advertising. Express the following as a ratio: time of advertising, in minutes, to time of actual program, in minutes.
Answer: _____

*Proportion*:  is an expression of two equal ratios.

> Example:  $5:10 = 10:20$ or $\frac{5}{10} = \frac{10}{20}$

A proportion equation may be used to solve for an unknown quantity. To solve for n:

1. Determine the cross product: multiply the numerator of each fraction by the denominator of the other fraction.

2. Solve for n: divide both sides of the equation by the same value.

3. Validate your answer by substituting the value for n into the original equation.

Example: $6:12 = 9:n$
1. $6 \times n = 9 \times 12$
   $6n = 108$
2. $\frac{6n}{6} = \frac{108}{6}$
   $n = 18$
3. Validate:
   $6 \times 18 = 9 \times 12$
   $108 = 108$

## Exercise 4.2

Complete the following exercise without referring to the previous text and without the aid of a calculator. Correct using the answer guide.

Solve for n:

1. $2:3 = n:12$          2. $n:125 = 1:5$

3. $\frac{5}{7} = \frac{15}{n}$          4. $25:1 = 50:n$

5. $10:1 = 15:n$          6. $75:2 = 50:n$

7. $100:1 = 37:n$          8. $0.25:1 = 0.125:n$

9. $250:1\,000 = n:1$          10. $n:100 = 10:1\,000$

### Expressing Ratios as Fractions, Decimals, and Percents

A ratio may be expressed as a fraction, a decimal number, or a percent. To convert a ratio to a fraction:

1. Place the first digit in the ratio over the second digit.
2. Reduce the fraction to its lowest term.

Example: $2:50$ as a fraction
1. $\frac{2}{50}$
2. Lowest term: $\frac{1}{25}$

To convert a ratio to a decimal:
1. Express the ratio as a fraction.
2. Divide the numerator into the denominator.
3. Follow the rules for writing decimals.

Example: $1:15$ as a decimal
1. Express as a fraction: $\frac{1}{15}$
2. Divide: 1 divided by 15 = .066
3. Follow rules for writing decimals: 0.066

To convert a ratio to a percent, use one of the following options:

### Option A

1. Express the ratio as a fraction.
2. Multiply by 100.
3. Divide the numerator by the denominator.
4. Add the percent sign.

> Example: Express 1:20 as a percent
> 1. Express as a fraction: $\frac{1}{20}$
> 2. Multiply by 100: $\frac{100}{20}$
> 3. Divide: 100 divided by 20 = 5
> 4. Add percent sign: 5%

### Option B

1. Express the ratio as a fraction.
2. Convert the fraction to a decimal number by dividing the numerator by the denominator.
3. Multiply the decimal number by 100.
4. Add the percent sign.

> Example: Express 1:20 as a percent
> 1. Express as a fraction: $\frac{1}{20}$
> 2. Convert to decimal: 0.05
> 3. Multiply by 100: 0.05 × 100 = 5
> 4. Add percent sign: 5%

Similarly, a percent may be expressed as a ratio, since percent means "out of one hundred." To convert a percent to a ratio, place the percent over 100. Thus:

$$50\% = \frac{50}{100} \quad \text{or} \quad \frac{5}{10} \quad \text{or} \quad \frac{1}{2}$$

$$0.5\% = \frac{0.5}{100} \quad \text{or} \quad \frac{5}{1\,000} \quad \text{or} \quad \frac{1}{200}$$

## Exercise 4.3

Complete the following exercise without referring to the previous text and without the aid of a calculator. Correct using the answer guide.

Express the following ratios as fractions, decimals, and percents. Express fractions in the lowest terms and round decimal numbers to the nearest tenth.

| Ratio | Fraction | Decimal | Percent |
|---|---|---|---|
| 2 per 50 | 1. | 2. | 3. |
| 1 to 10 | 4. | 5. | 6. |
| 7 to 9 | 7. | 8. | 9. |
| 25:2 | 10. | 11. | 12. |
| 50:1 | 13. | 14. | 15. |
| 10 to 1 | 16. | 17. | 18. |

Express these percents as ratios:

19.  75% =                    20.  33.3% –

21.  50% –                    22.   0.5% =

# POST-TEST

## Instructions

1. Write the post-test without referring to any references and without the aid of a calculator.

2. Correct the post-test using the answer guide.

3. If your score is 100 percent, proceed to the next module.

4. If you don't achieve 100 percent accuracy, review the learning package in this module and rewrite the post-test. You may wish to seek further assistance through the references listed in the bibliography.

1. $3:7 = n:21$ $n =$

2. $\frac{n}{10} = \frac{4}{5} =$ $n =$

3. $1:10 = n:100$ $n =$

4. Of sixty-two students in psychology, twenty-three are male. What is the ratio of male students to female students?
Answer: _____

5. A hockey player scores three goals in seventeen shots. What is the ratio of goals to shots?
Answer: _____

6. Define the term *ratio*.


7. Define the term *proportion*.



8. There are twenty-eight patients on a particular ward. The ratio of staff to patients is one to four. How many staff members are on this ward?
Answer: _____

9. Express the following statement as a ratio:

    Each teaspoon contains ten units of Drug A.

Answer: _____

10. Is the following relationship a proportion?

    $6:32 = 24:100$    Yes or No

11. Express 0.9% as a ratio.

Express the following ratios as fractions, decimal numbers and percents. Express fractions in lowest terms and round off decimal numbers to the nearest tenth.

| Ratios | Fractions | Decimals | Percents |
|---|---|---|---|
| 1 to 1 | 12. | 13. | 14. |
| 2 to 3 | 15. | 16. | 17. |
| 1 per 1 000 | 18. | 19. | 20. |

YOUR SCORE:_____ %

100%     YES—proceed to the next module
NO—review this module

**Note:** if you had any errors on the post-test, analyze your areas of weakness here before reviewing the appropriate section of the module.

# Module 5: Systems of Measurement

## PRE-TEST

## Instructions

1. Write the pre-test without referring to any resources and without the aid of a calculator.

2. Correct the pre-test using the answer guide.

3. If your score is 100 percent, proceed to the next module.

4. If your don't achieve 100 percent accuracy, read the learning package in this module and complete the exercises, concentrating on your weak areas as diagnosed by your pre-test score.

In the SI system, what are the base units of:

|   | | name | abbreviation |
|---|---|---|---|
| 1. | length | | |
| 2. | weight (mass) | | |
| 3. | substance | | |

Give the numerical value for each prefix:

4. deci _____

5. centi _____

6. milli _____

7. nano _____

8. micro _____

9. kilo _____

Do the following conversions of SI units:

10. 1 g = _____ mg

11. 1 L = _____ mL

12. 10 mg = _____ g

13. 1 kg = _____ g

14. 1 mg = _____ g

15. 250 mL = _____ L

16. 40 g = _____ kg

17. 200 mg = _____ g

18. 0.3 g = _____ mg

19. 1 m = _____ cm

20. 250 cm = _____ m

21. 0.6 g = _____ mg

Convert the following household measurements to SI units:

   22.  2 fl oz= _____ mL        23.  1 tsp= _____ mL

   24.  3 kg= _____ lb            25.  6 ft= _____ cm

YOUR SCORE: _____ %

     100%     YES—proceed to the next module
                     NO—review this module

**Note:** if you had any errors on the pre-test, analyze your areas of weakness here.

# Learning Package

```
                    Objective 5
         To convert between the base
         units and subunits of the S.I.
         system of measurement;
         to convert selected units of
         measurement from the S.I. sys-
         tem to other systems of meas-
         urement
```

## Systems of Measurement

In the past, pharmacology has relied on several systems of measurement that have made dosage calculations quite confusing. This confusion has contributed to medication errors. Today the movement is towards standardization. All drugs should be ordered and dispensed in S.I. units. Drug orders should be written in units called *grams, milligrams,* and *millilitres.* Nurses should not have to do conversions from one system of measurement to another, except for a few instances involving liquid medications, such as laxatives or antacids, or for instructions to the patient and family regarding uses of over-the-counter (OTC) drugs.

**Note:** if you are unfamiliar with any drug order written in non-standardized units, consult with the prescribing physician or a pharmacist. Presently in Canada, the nursing exams still use all three systems of measurement.

The major systems of measurement that have been used in pharmacology are:

### Household System

This system uses measures such as *drops, teaspoons,* and *tablespoons.* These measurements are most frequently used for prescription medications taken in the home and with such drugs as eye medications in the hospital. Figure 5.1 illustrates some household measures.

### Apothecaries' System

This is a very old system whose basic units include *minims, ounces,* and *grains.* These measures have become almost obsolete except for some drug orders for laxatives, antacids, and cough syrups that may be written in ounces.* It's useful for you to be familiar with some of the units of these systems, since patients and families might be accustomed to these measures.** However, the official system of measurement in Canada is the SI system, and therefore emphasis is placed on this system in the module.

* Also some aspirin products, which are still labelled in grains.
** *Pounds* and *inches* are also part of this system for example.

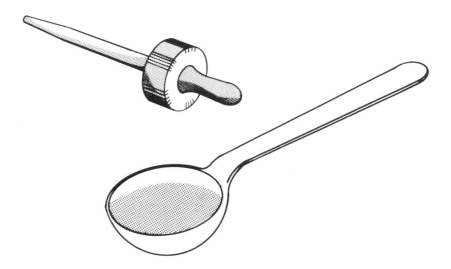

**Figure 5.1**  Household measures.

## SI System

The SI system, or Le Système international d'unités, is essentially an expanded version of the metric system. It is a decimal system based on the number ten.

There are seven base units or building blocks in this system. The *base units* you will encounter most often in relation to medications are outlined in Table 5-A.

**Table 5-A: Common Base Units**

| Name | Unit | Symbol |
|------|------|--------|
| metre | unit of length | m |
| kilogram | unit of mass | kg |
| mole | unit of substance | mol |

**Note:** Kilogram is the base unit not gram as in the metric system.

You are probably familiar with *metre* and *kilogram*. You've no doubt bought a metre of fabric or driven 100 kilometres. A metre is approximately the height of a doorknob. Possibly you have bought a kilogram of meat. A kilogram is approximately equal in weight of a one-litre carton of milk.

A *mole* is probably unfamiliar to you. It isn't a measurement of weight. A mole is an "amount of substance" defined as the number of atoms in exactly 12 g of the carbon-12 isotope. The number of entities in a mole of substance is $6.02 \times 10^{23}$. If your curiosity is aroused by this definition you might appreciate further explanation. An anonymous and creative author described one mole of peas as follows:

$10^{23}$ average-size peas would cover 250 planets the size of Earth with a blanket of peas one metre deep!

Obviously, one mole of peas occupies a much larger volume than a mole of potassium electrolytes.

Chemistry reports are expressed in molar units. This will become more significant to you when you read drug plasma levels reported in moles.

```
Examples:
insulin:   30 - 170 pmol/L
              (picomoles per litre)
digoxin:   <2.6 nmol/L
              (nanomoles per litre)
lithium:   0.6 - 1.2 mmol/L
              (millimoles per litre)
```

**Note:** Laboratory values can vary slightly. Check the normal values written on the lab reports in your particular clinical setting.

In addition to these base units, there is one other measurement that is not official SI but is of interest to health professionals. This is the unit of volume called the *litre*. For example, intravenous fluids are packaged in litre, 1 000 millilitre, containers.

Because the metre, kilogram, mole, and litre are relatively large units, the SI system uses prefixes to denote multiples and subunits. There are 16 prefixes, but only those used most frequently in relation to drug therapy are written in Table 5-B.

These numerical values are very important when converting base units and subunits of the SI system. You will do this frequently when administering medications and intravenous fluids to your patients. This module is an important step towards competence in calculating dosages.

**Table 5-B: SI Subunits**

| Prefix | Symbol | Numerical Value |
| --- | --- | --- |
| kilo | k | 1 000 |
| hecto | h | 100 |
| deci | d | 0.1 |
| centi | c | 0.01 |
| milli | m | 0.001 |
| micro | $\mu$ | 0.000 001 |
| nano | n | 0.000 000 001 |
| pico | p | 0.000 000 000 001 |

**Note:** the official symbol for *micro* is $\mu$; however, some references use mc. Both abbreviations are acceptable.

## Exercise 5.1

Review Table 5-B. Complete the following exercise without referring to the previous text. Correct using the answer guide.

What is the SI symbol for each of the following prefixes:

1.  kilo

2.  deci

3.  centi

4.  milli

5.  micro

Write out the numerical value for each of the following prefixes:

6.  kilo

7.  nano

8.  pico

9.  milli

10.  micro

11.  centi

12.  Name the 8 subunits of the SI system, as outlined in Table 5-B, from largest to smallest:

## Rules for Writing SI Symbols

1. Symbols of units are written in lower-case initials, except when they are named after a person.

> Example:
> degree Celsius=C
> metre=m

2. Symbols are not pluralized. They are also always written without a period, except when the symbol occurs at the end of a sentence.

> Example:
> He weighs 10 kg.
> Ten kg is correct.

3. Decimals should be used instead of fractions.

> Example:
> $\frac{1}{2}$ is 0.5

4. Always place a zero before the decimal point when there is no whole number.

> Example:
> 0.5 not .5

5. Just when you think you've got this mastered ... there's an exception to the rules. To avoid confusion with the number 1, write the word *litre* in full or use capital *L*. The capital *L* is also used with prefixes.

> Example:
> litre = L
> millilitre = mL

6. Writing numbers with more than three digits; that is, in the thousands, is slightly different from our traditional method. No comma is used. Instead a space is left, as shown in the example.

| Example: |
|---|
| 1 000.039 78 |
| 23 000 |
| 217 860 |

7. Because old habits die slowly, there is one other point you should know. Although cc, *cubic centimetre*, isn't a standard SI unit, it's frequently used by health professionals— especially those of us who are B.S.I.—before SI! The cc should be replaced by mL, millilitre. One, cc is approximately equal to 1 mL.

## Exercise 5.2

Complete the following exercise without referring to the previous text. Correct using the answer guide.

Indicate which of the following correctly adhere to the rules for writing SI symbols. Circle your choice.

1. metre = m or M

2. 10 kilograms = 10 kg or 10 kgs

3. $\frac{1}{2}$ millilitre = $\frac{1}{2}$ mL or 0.5 mL or 0.5 ml

4. litre = L or l

5. One thousand millilitres = 1 000 mL or 1,000 mL

6. Write fifty-one thousand, five hundred and seventeen according to the S.I. rules:

7. True or false? One cc is approximately equal to 1 mL.

## Converting SI Subunits to Base Units

The most common subunits encountered in drug therapy are *milli* and *micro*. In addition, you will frequently encounter *centi* in measurements of height or length. Table 5-C illustrates the relationship between units of the SI system.

**Table 5-C: Units and Subunits**

| Unit | Unit | Value |
|---|---|---|
| gram (g) *to* | milligram (mg) | 1 g = 1 000 mg |
| gram (g) *to* | microgram ($\mu$) | 1 g = 1 000 000 $\mu$g |
| litre (L) *to* | millilitre (mL) | 1 L = 1 000 mL |
| metre (m) *to* | centimetre (cm) | 1 m = 100 cm |
| metre (m) *to* | millimetre (mm) | 1 m = 1 000 mm |

Conversion of subunits to base units and vice versa is a very simple exercise, involving multiplication or division by 10, 100, or 1 000. The trick, of course, is to remember whether you should multiply or divide!

> **Example: convert g to mg**

Review Tables 5-B and 5-C. Recall that the gram is the base unit and that the prefix milli means a thousandth of the base unit; that is, 1 milligram is 0.001 grams. Milligram is a subunit of the base unit gram. Therefore:

> 1 g (gram) = 1 000 mg (milligrams)
> and
> 1 milligram = 0.001 grams.

> **Example: 10 g = ? mg**

Multiply the base unit by the subunit:

10 × 1 000 = 10 000

To multiply by 10, move the decimal point one place to the right. Alternatively, use ratio and proportion to solve:

$$1 \text{ g} = 1\ 000 \text{ mg}$$

$$10 \text{ g} = ? \text{ mg}$$

$$1{:}10 = 1\ 000{:}\ ?$$
$$\frac{1}{10} = \frac{1\ 000}{?}$$
$$? = 10\ 000$$
$$10 \text{ g} = 10\ 000 \text{ mg}$$

> **Example: 0.2 g = ? mg**

Multiply the base unit by the subunit:

0.2 × 1 000 = ?

Move the decimal point three places to the right:

0.2 × 1 000 = 200

Therefore, 0.2 g = 200 mg

Alternatively, use ratio and proportion to solve:

> If 1 g = 1 000 mg,
>
> then 0.2 g = ? mg
>
> 1:1 000 = 0.2:?
>
> ? = 200

In these examples, you know the base unit and you are looking for the subunits. What about the reverse, when you know the number of subunits and you want to convert to the base unit?

$$\boxed{\text{Example:}250 \text{ mg } = ? \text{ g}}$$

In this example, write the problem according to Option A or Option B and then use ratio proportion to solve.

**Option A**    1 mg = 0.001 g

250 mg = ? g

1:250 = 0.001:?

$\frac{1}{250} = \frac{0.001}{?}$

? = 250 × 0.001

? = .250

Write according to the rules:

? = 0.25

250 mg = 0.25 g

**Option B**    250 mg = ? g

1 000:250 = 1:?

$\frac{1\,000}{250} = \frac{1}{?}$

$? = \frac{250}{1\,000}$

? = .250

Write according to the rules:

? = 0.25

250 mg = 0.25 g

## Exercise 5.3

Complete the following exercise without referring to the previous text and without the aid of a calculator. Correct using the answer guide.

1.  1 L = _____ mL
2.  1 kg = _____ g
3.  1 m = _____ cm
4.  1 cc = _____ mL
5.  1 g = _____ $\mu$g
6.  250 mL = _____ L
7.  0.5 g = _____ mg
8.  2 m = _____ cm
9.  1 mg = _____ $\mu$g
10. 1 000 $\mu$g = _____ g
11. 300 mg = _____ g
12. 800 g = _____ kg
13. 150 cm = _____ m
14. 0.75 g = _____ mg
15. 2 500 g = _____ kg

## Common Conversions

Because of the common usage of inches, pounds, and fluid ounces by the public and professionals, it is practical to know the following conversions from the SI system to the household and apothecaries' systems. Table 5-D lists these common conversions.

### Table 5-D: Common Conversions

| Unit | SI | Household/Apothecaries |
|------|-----|------------------------|
| weight | kg<br>1 kg = | pounds<br>2.2 pounds (lbs) |
| height | cm<br>2.54 cm = | inches<br>1 inch |
| volume | mL<br>30 mL = | fluid ounces<br>1 ounce (oz) |
|        | mL<br>4-5 mL = | teaspoon<br>1 teaspoon (tsp) |

How do you convert kilograms to pounds or teaspoons to millilitres?

> Example:  2 kg = ? lb
> Multiply by 2.2: 2 × 2.2 = 4.4 lbs
>
> Example:  88 lb = ? kg
> Divide by 2.2
> 88 ÷ 2.2 = 40 kg
>
> Example:  3 oz = ? mL
> Multiply by 30: 3 × 30 = 90 mL

## Exercise 5.4

Review Table 5-D and master the conversions before completing the following exercise. Answer the questions without referring back to Table 5-D. Correct using the answer guide.

You are admitting Mr. Jones, who cannot be weighed. He tells you his weight is 175 lb.

1. Convert this to kg.


2. Round off to the nearest tenth.


3. Round off to the nearest kg.


Tim's height is 140 cm.

4. Express Tim's height in inches.


5. Express Tim's height in feet and inches.


6. The label states: "For ages 2 to 3, give 1 tsp."
Convert this measurement to mL.


7. The order is: Magnolax 1 oz. Convert to mL.

# POST-TEST

## Instructions

1. Write the post-test without referring to any reference materials and without the aid of a calculator.

2. Correct the post-test using the answer guide.

3. If your score is 100 percent, proceed to the next module.

4. If you don't achieve 100 percent, review the appropriate sections of the learning package in this module and rewrite the post-test. You may wish to seek further assistance through the references listed in the bibliography.

1.   2 L           =      _____ mL

2.   250 mg        =      _____ g

3.   2 000 mg      =      _____ g

4.   6 g           =      _____ mg

5.   7 kg          =      _____ g

6.   5 000 mL      =      _____ L

7.   1.25 mg       =      _____ g

8.   0.003 g       =      _____ mg

9.   2.5 g         =      _____ mg

10.  0.5 L         =      _____ mL

11.  1 456 g       =      _____ kg

12.  0.5 mg        =      _____ g

13.  1 mg          =      _____ µg

14.  1.7 m         =      _____ cm

15.  179 cm        =      _____ m

16.  0.5 g         =      _____ mg

17.  250 mL        =      _____ L

18.  1.34 g        =      _____ mg

19.  10 g          =      _____ µg

20.  79 kg         =      _____ mg

Give the numerical value for each prefix:

21. centi

22. milli

23. micro

24. kilo

25. deci


YOUR SCORE:_____ %

100%    YES—proceed to the next module
NO—review this module

___

**Note:** if you had any errors on the post-test, analyze your areas of weakness before reviewing the module.

# Module 6: Reading Medication Orders and Labels

## PRE-TEST

### Instructions

1. Write the pre-test without referring to any resources and without the aid of a calculator.

2. Correct the pre-test using the answer guide.

3. If your score is 100 percent, proceed to the next module.

4. If you don't achieve 100 percent accuracy, read the learning package in this module and complete the exercises, concentrating on your weak areas as diagnosed by your pre-test score.

Interpret each of the following medication orders and write out the underlined abbreviation in full.

1. Morphine sulfate 10–15 mg I.M. q.4h. p.r.n.

2. Insulin 6 units S.C. stat.

3. Metoclopramide (Reglan) 10 mg P.O. a.c. t.i.d.

4. Aluminum hydroxide 30 mL P.O. 1 hour p.c. t.i.d.

5. Flurazepam hydrochloride (Dalmane) 15 mg P.O. h.s.

Refer to Figure 6.1 and answer questions 6 and 7.

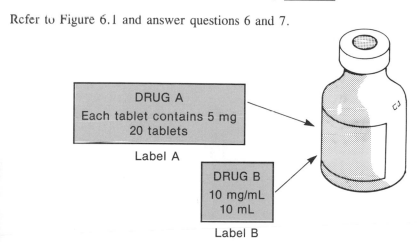

DRUG A
Each tablet contains 5 mg
20 tablets

Label A

DRUG B
10 mg/mL
10 mL

Label B

**Figure 6.1**  Drug labels A and B

|  | Label | |
|---|---|---|
| | A | B |
| 6. form of the drug | | |
| 7. dosage strength | | |

List the parts of a medication order. All medication orders should include the patient, the drug name, the frequency or time of administration, and the

8. d_____ ,

9. and r_____ .

10. A single-dose ampule labelled 25 mg/mL contains exactly 1 mL of liquid. True or false?

Match the abbreviation in column 1 with the correct expression in column 2.

| Column 1 | Column 2 |
|---|---|
| 11. _____ p.c. | A. twice daily |
| 12. _____ stat. | B. capsule |
| 13. _____ elix. | C. ointment |
| 14. _____ ung. | D. at bedtime |
| 15. _____ tab. | E. after meals |
| 16. _____ a.c. | F. elixir |
| 17. _____ cap. | G. immediately |
| 18. _____ b.i.d. | H. tablet |
| 19. _____ h.s. | I. before meals |
| 20. _____ S.C. | J. subcutaneous |

YOUR SCORE: _____ %

100%     YES—proceed to the next module
         NO—complete this module

**Note:** if you had any errors on the pre-test, analyze your areas of weakness here.

# Learning Package

---

### Objective 6

**To interpret medication orders; to determine concentrations of liquid medications and describe the reconstitution of powdered drugs**

---

## Medication Orders

In most clinical settings, medications are prescribed by a physician, dispensed by a pharmacist, and administered by a nurse. All medication orders should include the patient's name, the drug, dose, route, and frequency or time of administration.

---

Example:   morphine sulfate 10 mg I.M. stat
           drug    dose    route    time  or  frequency

---

Obviously this order would also specify the recipient!

**Note:** dose and dosage both refer to the exact amount of medicine to be given or taken at a specified time.

### Commonly Used Abbreviations

The first step is correct interpretation of the medication order. Handwriting jokes aside, even a legible order is usually written in shorthand. It's important to learn this "new language." Abbreviations vary considerably among institutions and prescribers. Some are easily misinterpreted and can lead to error. For example, q.d., o.d., OD, have all been used to mean "daily" or "once a day". However, OD also means "right eye". The abbreviation, q.d., can also be confused with q.i.d., which would result in a very serious error. For example, digoxin (Lanoxin) would be given four times a day instead of only once. The letter "u for units" can be easily misread as a *0*. For example, serious drug errors have occurred because 6 u of insulin was read as 60. The abbreviations listed in Table 6–A have become widely accepted. Some have been used in the calculation problems in this workbook. The reader is urged to verify acceptable abbreviations used in the practice setting.

## Table 6–A: Commonly Used Abbreviations

| | |
|---|---|
| a.c. | before meals ($\frac{1}{2}$ hour before meals) |
| b.i.d. | twice daily |
| cap. | capsule |
| elix. | elixir |
| ext. | extract |
| h.s. | at bedtime |
| I.M. or i.m. | intramuscular |
| I.V. or i.v. | intravenous |
| mEq. | milliequivalent |
| p.c. | after meals ($\frac{1}{2}$ hour after meals) |
| P.O. or p.o. | by mouth |
| p.r.n. | as necessary (according to necessity) |
| q.h. | every hour |
| q.4h. | every four hours |
| q.i.d. | four times a day |
| q.s. | as much as required |
| S.C. or s.c. | subcutaneous |
| stat. | immediately |
| tab. | tablet |
| t.i.d. | three times a day |
| u. | unit |
| ung. | ointment |

**Note:** sometimes these abbreviations are written without periods; for example, bid, po.
Unit: a drug measure based on a specific effect; such as, a unit of insulin is a standardized amount that lowers blood sugar.
Milliequivalent: measurement of combining power rather than weight.

## Exercise 6.1

Complete the following exercise without referring to the previous text. Correct using the answer guide.

Interpret the following medication orders. Write out each of the underlined abbreviations in full.

1. Meperidine (Demerol) 50–75 mg I.M. q.3–4h. p.r.n.

2. Acetaminophen (Tylenol) 650 mg P.O. q.4h.

3. Codeine sulfate 60 mg P.O. stat and q.4h.

4. Penicillin 500 000 units I.V. q.i.d.

5. Phenobarbital elix. 100 mg h.s.

List the parts of a medication order:

6.                                        7.

8.                                        9.

10.

## Medication Labels

The medication label contains very important information. Some labels are clearly present-ed, provided your vision is satisfactory! Other labels are confusing. They aren't standardized as to what information is included or how it is presented. It's important to develop the habit of thoroughly studying the information and instructions on drug labels. Accompanying liter-ature also provides useful information. Check your habits: the last time you bought a piece of equipment—tape recorder, video machine, or pocket calculator—*did you read the in-structions*?

The label in Figure 6.2 illustrates the type of information that should be included in drug packaging.

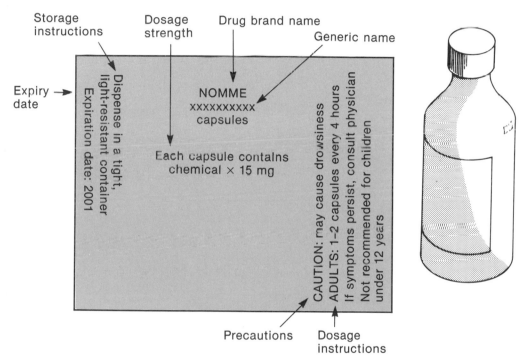

**Figure 6.2**  Drug Label Sample

## Exercise 6.2

Complete the following exercise without referring to the previous text. Correct using the answer guide.

Refer to Figure 6.3 and answer questions 1 to 12.

100 tablets
DRUG C
enteric coated
150 mg

Label C

100 mL
DRUG D
100 mg per 5 mL

Label D

Vial # 10 mL
DRUG E
1 000 μg
per mL

Label E

**Figure 6.3** Drug labels C, D, and E

**Answer Questions 1 to 12**

**Label C**

1. Form of the drug
2. Dosage strength
3. Total volume of container or total number of tablets
4. Total dosage of drug in container

**Label D**

5. Form of the drug
6. Dosage strength
7. Total volume of container or total number of tablets
8. Total amount of drug in container

**Label E**

9. Form of the drug
10. Dosage strength
11. Total volume of container or total number of tablets
12. Total amount of drug in container

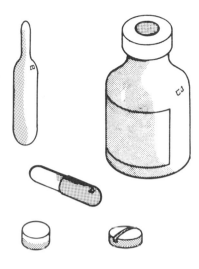

**Figure 6.4**  Dosage Forms

## Packaging of Medications

Medications are prepared and packaged in a variety of forms. Oral doses are provided in compressed tablets, capsules, and liquids. Injectables are packaged in both single-dose and multiple-dose containers. Figure 6.4 illustrates some of these forms.

Regarding the single-dose ampule, an important point should be made. The ampule may state that ? mg per mL are contained premixed for a single dose. However, the ampule contains slightly greater than one mL, to allow for some loss of solution within the needle and syringe. Therefore, always carefully calculate and measure the correct dose and do not draw up the entire contents of an ampule. A similar point can be made regarding vials and bags of intravenous fluids. All packages of liquid medication contain extra fluid.

Injectables are prepared as liquids ready for injection or in powdered form requiring reconstitution with a diluent. The procedure for reconstitution and calculation of these products is described in Module 7.

Now let's interpret the medication order and read a drug label.

> Example: the physician orders
> Drug E 1 200 $\mu$g I.M. today.

You go to the medication cart and discover the multiple-dose vial described in Figure 6.3. The label tells you that you do, indeed, have Drug E in a concentration of 1 000 $\mu$g per mL. Now you must calculate the correct dosage. Module 7 will teach you the rules. (For your own interest and curiosity, how would you solve this problem right now?)

# POST-TEST

## Instructions

1. Write the post-test without referring to any reference materials.

2. Correct the post-test using the answer guide.

3. If your score is 100 percent, proceed to the next module.

4. If you don't achieve 100 percent, review the learning package in this module and re-write the post-test. You may wish to seek further assistance through the reference listed in the bibliography.

### *Part One*

Complete the crossword in Figure 6.5 with the correct abbreviation. (Value: 16)

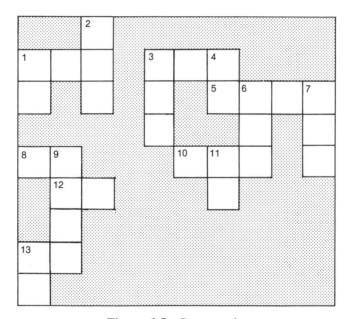

**Figure 6.5**   Crossword

Across

1. as required
3. every 4 hours
5. immediately
8. after meals
10. twice daily
12. before meals
13. as much as is required

Down

1. by mouth
2. ointment
3. four times a day
4. at bedtime
6. three times a day
7. tablet
9. capsules
11. intramuscular
13. every hour

*Part Two*

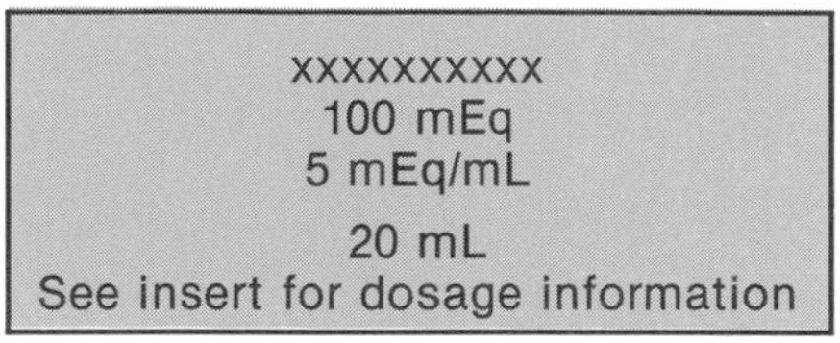

XXXXXXXXXX
100 mEq
5 mEq/mL

20 mL
See insert for dosage information

**Figure 6.6**  Drug Label

Read the label in Figure 6.6 to answer the following questions. (Value: 4)

a. What is the form of the drug?

b. What is the total volume in the container?

c. What is the concentration of the drug?

d. What is the total amount of drug in this container?

YOUR SCORE: _____ %

100%      YES—proceed to the next module
          NO—review this module

---

**Note:** if you had any errors on the post-test, analyze your areas of weakness here before reviewing the appropriate section of the module.

# Module 7: Dosage Calculations

## PRE-TEST

### Instructions

1. Write the pre-test without referring to any resource materials and without the aid of a calculator.

2. Correct the pre-test using the answer guide.

3. If your score is 100 percent, proceed to the next module.

4. If you don't achieve 100 percent accuracy, read the learning package in this module and complete the exercises, concentrating on your weak areas as diagnosed by your pre-test score.

Calculate the following doses to be administered:

**Note:** be careful to include the appropriate unit of measurement with your answer, e.g., tablet, mg, mL. Round off decimal numbers to nearest hundredth.

1. The order is: heparin 8 000 units intravenous stat. The vial is labelled: 10 000 units per mL. Determine the correct dose in mL.

2. The order is: 0.015 g of Drug X. The tablets are 5 mg each. Determine the correct dose in tablets.

3. From aspirin tablets of 325 mg each, determine the correct dose in tablets for 650 mg P.O.

4. The penicillin vial is labelled: 200 000 units/mL. The order is: 80 000 units I.M. Determine the correct dose in mL.

5. The order is: cephalexin (Keflex) 1 g P.O. q.6h. The bottle is labelled: 500 mg tablets. Determine the correct dose in tablets.

6. The patient is to receive theophylline (Theodur) 450 mg P.O. p.c. The drug is available in 300 mg scored tablets. Determine the correct dose in tablets.

7. The order is: bromocriptine mesylate (Parlodel) 5 mg P.O. daily. The available form is 2.5 mg tablets. Determine the correct dose in tablets.

8. The order is: nadolol (Corgard) 40 mg P.O. h.s. The scored tablets are available in 80-mg strength. Determine the correct dose in tablets.

9. The patient is to receive levothyroxine sodium (Synthroid) 0.15 mg P.O. once daily. The bottle is labelled: Synthroid 0.05 mg/tablet. Determine the correct dose in tablets.

Read the following order and answer questions 10, 11, and 12.

The order is:  NPH insulin 22 units S.C. q.am. regular insulin 12 units S.C. q.am. The vials are labelled:  NPH 100 units/mL and regular insulin 100 units/mL.

10.  Determine the correct dose of NPH in mL

11.  Determine the correct dose of regular insulin in mL

12.  Determine the total dose of insulin (the two insulins can be mixed in the same syringe)

13.  The order is:  perphenazine (Trilafon) 3.5 mg I.M. stat. The ampule is labelled:  5 mg/mL. Determine the correct dose in mL.

14.  The order is:  digoxin (Lanoxin) 0.125 mg P.O. q.am. The bottle is labelled:  digoxin 0.25 mg tablets. Determine the correct dose in tablets.

15.  From hydrocortisone (Solucortef) 100 mg/2 mL, determine the correct dose for 75 mg I.M. daily.

16.  The order is:  cloxacillin sodium (Orbenin) 500 mg q.i.d. × 21 days. The available form is 250 mg capsules. How many capsules will be required for a 21-day supply?

17.  The order is:  meperidine (Demerol) 75 mg I.M. p.r.n. The ampule is labelled:  meperidine 100 mg/mL. Determine the correct dose in mL.

For each of the following situations in questions 18–22, indicate whether there are errors in the calculations or in the written form of the answer:

18.  The order is:  heparin 5 000 units S.C. b.i.d. Available is heparin 10 000 units/mL. The correct dose to administer subcutaneously is:  .5 mL

19.  The order is:  dimenhydrinate (Gravol) 50 mg I.M. stat. A single-dose ampule is labelled:  50 mg/mL. The correct dose to administer intramuscularly is:  1 ampule

20.  Fluphenazine decanoate (Modecate) 12.5 mg I.M. is ordered. The vial is labelled:  10 mL of Modecate 25 mg/mL. The correct dose to administer is:  2 mL.

21.  The order is:  indomethacin (Indocid) 25 mg P.O. The drug is available in 25 mg capsules. The correct dose to administer is:  1 capsule

22. A colleague asks you to double-check the heparin dose. The order is for 4 300 units I.V. by continuous infusion. The heparin is labelled: 1 000 units/mL. Your colleague has drawn up 4 mL of heparin into a syringe. Is this correct?

23. You must administer 300 000 units of an antibiotic by I.M. injection. The label instructions state: "add 5 mL of bacteriostatic water to yield 500 000 units per mL." Calculate the amount to give.

24. The order states: ampicillin 1 g I.V. q.6h., and the dose on hand is a vial of powdered medication. The label reads: 1 000 mg. If you add 1 mL of bacteriostatic water to the vial, calculate the dosage you will administer.

25. A multiple-dose vial containing a powdered antibiotic is labelled: Drug Q 10 g. The instructions state: "add 7.2 mL of sterile water to yield 10 mL total volume." What is the concentration in g per mL?

YOUR SCORE: _____ %

100%    YES—proceed to the next module
NO—complete this module

**Note:** if you had any errors on the pre-test, analyze your areas of weakness here.

## Learning Package

---

**Objective 7**
**To accurately calculate dos-
ages of oral and parenteral
medications**

---

The previous modules presented a review of basic arithmetic skills: addition, subtraction, multiplication, and division of whole numbers, decimal numbers, and fractions. These skills are required for accurate dosage calculations.

**Note:** the terms *dose* and *dosage* can be used interchangeably. Each term means the amount of medication to be given.

Frequently nurses must calculate and administer drugs or instruct patients and families in calculations for self-medication. Accurate dosage calculation is extremely important to patient safety. This module describes a formula for calculating oral and parenteral medications, as well as providing several practice exercises to develop your skill. If you don't like to remember formulas, an alternate method using ratio and proportion is also described.

## Calculating Dosages of Tablets

The oral route is the most common route of drug administration. To calculate the number of tablets or capsules, the formula is:

$$\frac{\text{dose desired}}{\text{dose on hand}} = \frac{\text{number of tablets}}{\text{to administer}}$$

Sometimes the dose ordered and the dose on hand are in the same unit of measurement.

---

Example:

The physician orders ascorbic acid 100 mg P.O.
The dose on hand is in 50 mg tablets.

$$\frac{\text{dose desired}}{\text{dose on hand}} = \frac{100 \text{ mg}}{50 \text{ mg}} = 2 \text{ tabs}$$

The correct dosage to administer is 2 tablets.

---

In other situations, the dose desired and the dose on hand are in different units.

> Example:
>
> The order is for 1.5 g of sulfisoxazole (Gantrisin).
> Available: 500 mg tablets.
>
> Note: The dose desired and the dose on hand must be written in the same units.
>
> Step 1: convert the order to the same unit as the dose on hand. (Review Module 5 if necessary.)
>
> 1.5 g = ? mg
>
> = 1 500 mg
>
> Step 2: use the formula.
>
> $$\frac{\text{dose desired}}{\text{dose on hand}} = \frac{1\ 500\ mg}{500\ mg}$$
>
> 1 500 divided by 500 = 3
>
> The correct dosage to administer is 3 tablets.

For those of you who prefer to solve dosage calculations using ratio and proportion, the following example illustrates this method of problem solving.

> Example:
>
> The order is for diazepam (Valium) 5 mg P.O.
> The bottle is labelled: diazepam 10 mg tablets.
>
> Known ratio: 10 mg/1 tablet
>
> Unknown ratio: 5 mg/? tablets
>
> 5 mg:? tab = 10 mg:1 tab
>
> $$\frac{5}{?} = \frac{10}{1}$$
>
> $$? = \frac{5}{10}$$
>
> $? = 0.5$ or $\frac{1}{2}$ tablet
>
> Give $\frac{1}{2}$ a tablet

**Note:** always check your answer "intuitively". Does it make sense?

In the previous example, 5 mg were ordered. This is *less* than the amount available. This answer does make sense.

## Exercise 7.1

Complete the following exercise without referring to the previous text and without the aid of a calculator. Correct using the answer guide. Be *careful* to state your answer in full: include tablets, capsules, or other pill forms in your response.

1. On hand are sulfisoxazole (Gantrisin) tablets of 500 mg each. How many tablets are required for a single dose of 1 g?

2. The order is: sulfisoxazole (Gantrisin) 1.5 g P.O. t.i.d. The available strength is 500 mg/tablet. Determine the correct amount to administer.

3. The order is: caffeine 0.2 g p.r.n. The tablets are labelled 100 mg each. Determine the correct amount to administer.

4. You are to give meperidine (Demerol) 75 mg P.O. for pain. The scored tablets on hand are 50 mg each. Determine the correct amount to administer.

5. The order is: hydrochlorothiazide (Hydrodiuril) 100 mg P.O. daily. The available tablets are labelled: 50 mg each. Determine the correct amount to administer.

6. The patient is to receive 30 mg P.O. of Drug A. There are two dosage strengths available. One bottle is labelled: 5 mg tablets, and another bottle contains 20 mg tablets. Determine the correct amount to administer. Be certain to indicate which tablet strength you are using.

7. The order is: digoxin (Lanoxin) 0.125 mg P.O. daily. The available scored tablets are 0.25 mg strength. Determine the correct amount to administer.

8. The order is: levothyroxine sodium (Eltroxin) 0.1 mg P.O. daily. The tablets are labelled 0.05 mg each. Determine the correct amount to administer.

9. The patient is to receive 0.05 mg of Drug B. The scored tablets are labelled 0.1 mg each. Determine the correct amount to administer.

10. The order is for 0.5 g of an antibiotic. The bottle is labelled 250 mg capsules. Determine the correct amount to administer.

## Calculating Dosages of Liquids

Many medications are administered orally in suspensions and parenterally in solutions. Consider the following situation:

> Example:
>
> The order is: thioridazine hydrochloride (Mellaril) 60 mg P.O. p.r.n.
> On hand is Mellaril 25 mg/5mL. What amount should be administered?

Obviously the answer must be expressed in volume. How many mL should the patient receive? Our previous formula can be used with slight modification.

$$\frac{\text{dose desired}}{\text{dose on hand}} \times \text{volume} = \frac{\text{volume to}}{\text{administer}}$$

> Example: in the previous example, the dose desired is 60 mg and the dose on hand is 25 mg in 5 mL.
>
> $$\frac{60 \text{ mg}}{25 \text{ mg}} \times 5 \text{ mL}$$
>
> Answer: 12 mL

Dosage errors are often due to carelessness. Whenever you calculate a dosage, check the answer to see if it seems reasonable. For example, in this previous problem would an answer of 1 mL seem reasonable?

Alternatively, you can also solve this problem using ratio and proportion. Once again you have a known ratio and an unknown ratio.

> Known ratio: 25 mg/5 mL
> Unknown ratio: 60 mg/? mL
> 60 mg:? mL = 25 mg:5 mL
> $$\frac{60 \text{ mg}}{? \text{ mL}} = \frac{25 \text{ mg}}{5 \text{ mL}}$$
> 25 ? = 300
> ? = 12

Check that each side of the equation expresses the same relationship; that is, mg to mL.

Note: be certain to express the units of weight and volume in your ratio. It's easy to come up with an answer and then be left wondering...
? = 12 (but 12 what? mg? mL?)
Place "12" in the original equation, and you know the answer is 12 mL.

Before studying the calculation of liquid medications for parenteral administration you should be familiar with the calibration of syringes. This module does not acquaint you with the procedure of using a syringe for injection. Examine the figures only to become familiar with the calibration of each. Figure 7.1 illustrates a 2 $\frac{1}{2}$-mL syringe that is calibrated in 0.1 mL units. Figure 7.2 illustrates a 1-mL, or 1-cc, syringe that is calibrated in 0.01 mL units. Recall from Module 5 that mL = cc. If you aren't familiar with syringes, study the illustrations in Figure 7.1 and Figure 7.2.

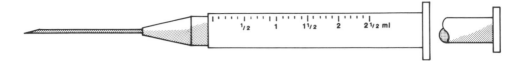

**Figure 7.1**   $2\frac{1}{2}$-mL syringe

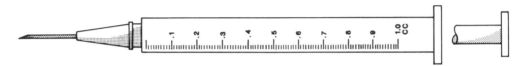

**Figure 7.2**   1–mL or 1–cc syringe

The following example illustrates the calculation of a liquid medication for parenteral administration.

> Example:
>
> Ordered:   110 units of Drug M
> Available:   Drug M 100 units/mL
> Calculate:   $\dfrac{110 \text{ units}}{100 \text{ units}} \times 1 \text{ mL} = 1.1 \text{ mL}$

Figure 7.3 illustrates 1.1 mL in a $2\frac{1}{2}$-mL syringe. Note that this syringe is also calibrated in minims, an Apothecaries' measurement.

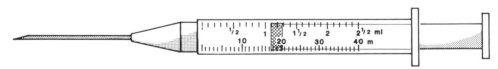

**Figure 7.3**   $2\frac{1}{2}$-mL syringe filled to 1.1 mL

## Exercise 7.2

Complete the following exercise without referring to the previous text and without the aid of a calculator. Correct using the answer guide. Be *careful* to include the appropriate units in your answer. State decimal numbers in the nearest hundredth.

1.  The order is:  heparin 7 500 units S.C. You have a 5-mL vial of heparin labelled:  10 000 units/mL. Determine the correct dosage to administer.

2.  The label on a 2-mL ampule indicates 50 mg/mL. How many mg are contained in 1.5 mL?

3.  The order is: 20 mEq KCl elixir b.i.d. The bottle is labelled ''each 15 mL contains 1.5 g (20 mEq) of potassium chloride''. Determine the correct dosage to administer.

4. Your patient has an order for meperidine (Demerol) 75 mg I.M. The 2-mL ampule is labelled: 50 mg/mL. How many mL should the patient receive?

5. The physician has ordered 0.1 mg of Medication A. The ampule is labelled: Medication A: 0.25 mg in 5 mL. Determine the correct dosage to administer.

For each of the following questions, shade in the accompanying syringe to indicate the correct dosage.

6. Ordered: heparin 5 000 units S.C.
   On hand: heparin sodium 10 000 units/mL.

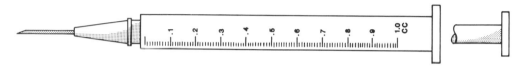

**Figure 7.4**   amount of heparin

7. Ordered: NPH insulin 37 units.
   On hand: NPH insulin 100 units/mL.

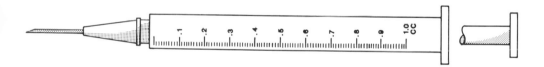

**Figure 7.5**   amount of NPH insulin

8. Ordered: morphine 15 mg I.M.
   perphenazine (Trilafon) 3.5 mg.
   On hand: morphine 15 mg/mL.
   perphenazine 5 mg/mL.

These two drugs can be mixed in the same syringe. Calculate the total amount.

**Figure 7.6**   amount of morphine and perphenazine

9. Ordered: dimenhydrinate (Gravol) 30 mg I.M. p.r.n.
On hand: 50 mg/mL.

**Figure 7.7**   amount of dimenhydrinate

10. An analgesic is ordered: 75 mg I.M. stat. On hand is a 2-mL ampule with a dosage concentration of 50 mg/mL. Calculate the dose to administer.

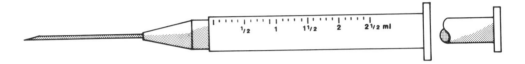

**Figure 7.8**   amount of analgesic

## Reconstituting Medications

To increase their stability, some medications are prepared in a dry powder form and must be diluted with a sterile solvent before administration. For example, many antibiotics must be reconstituted with sterile water. Refer to Table 7–A, which illustrates a dilution table on a multiple-dose vial. Note that adding 46 mL of sterile diluent yields a solution with 200 000 I.U. (International Units) of medication in each millilitre. Contrast this concentration with the solution that results when only 6 mL of diluent, usually sterile water, are added.

When a certain volume of liquid is added to a powdered drug in a vial, the resulting product will be of a greater volume. For example, in the previous product, adding 9.3 mL of fluid may result in a final volume in the vial of 10 mL. The powdered drug occupies some volume.

**Table 7–A: Dilution**

| Potency Required I.U. per mL | Add Sterile Aqueous Diluent |
|---|---|
| 200 000 | 46 mL |
| 250 000 | 36 mL |
| 750 000 | 9.3 mL |
| 1 000 000 | 6 mL |

## Examples of Reconstituting Medications

Because reconstituting medications presents some confusing situations, two examples are presented here followed by an exercise for practice.

Example 1: The label on a single-dose vial containing a powdered medication states: 500 mg. To administer a dosage of 500 mg, you would add a small volume of solvent—usually sterile distilled water, unless otherwise instructed on the label—rotate or invert several times to dissolve the powder thoroughly, then administer the entire contents of the ampule. It's customary to add 1 mL of liquid. However, remember that the final volume may be slightly more than 1 mL due to the volume of the powder.

Example 2: The label on a multiple-dose vial containing a powdered medication states: 5 000 000 units. The label instructions for preparation of solution are:

| Add diluent | Concentration of solution |
|---|---|
| 18 mL | 250 000 units/mL |
| 8 mL | 500 000 units/mL |
| 3 mL | 1 000 000 units/mL |

The order states: 400 000 units I.M. q.i.d.

Step 1: determine the volume of solvent or diluent

In this example you want a concentrated solution for I.M. injection. However, you also want sufficient diluent to ensure adequate mixing of the suspension and absorption of the drug. Let's add 8 mL of diluent, sterile water for injection. Be *certain* to indicate the concentration strength you have prepared directly on the label for further doses!

Step 2: invert or rotate several times to dissolve medication thoroughly

Step 3: calculate the amount required

$$\frac{\text{dose desired}}{\text{dose on hand}} \times \text{volume} = ?$$

$$\frac{400\ 000\ \text{units}}{500\ 000\ \text{units}} \times 1\ \text{mL} = 0.8\ \text{mL}$$

## Exercise 7.3

Refer to the vial label illustrated in Table 7–A to answer the following questions. Correct using the answer guide. Express decimal numbers to the nearest hundredth.

1. The order is for 750 000 units I.V. q.4h. How much diluent would you add to yield a solution with a concentration of 750 000 units/mL?

2. The medication has been mixed by another nurse, and the vial is signed, dated, and marked to indicate that 9.3 mL of sterile diluent was added. How much would be required to administer a dose of 1 million units?

You add 46 mL of sterile diluent and mix the powdered drug. For each of the following orders, in questions 3–5 indicate the correct dosage to administer:

3. 750 000 units

4. 400 000 units

5. 250 000 units

You add 9.3 mL of sterile diluent and mix the powdered drug. For each of the following volumes, in questions 6–8 indicate the amount of drug, in units:

6. 1 mL

7. 0.8 mL

8. 1.4 mL

A multiple-dose vial states that it contains 10 g of Drug T. The instructions: "add 7.2 mL of sterile water to yield 10 mL of solution".

9. What is the total volume of solution in this vial?

10. If the order is for 1 g I.V., how many doses can be given from this vial?

Because of the importance of competence in dosage calculation, an additional exercise is provided in this module. This exercise also encourages you to recall information from Module 6.

## Exercise 7.4

Answer the following questions without referring to the previous text and without the aid of a calculator. Correct using the answer guide. Be *careful* to express your answers in the appropriate units. Round off decimal numbers to the nearest hundredth.

1. Ordered: morphine sulfate 7.5 mg I.M. p.r.n. for pain.
   Available: ampule labelled morphine 10 mg/mL.
   Amount to give?

2. Ordered: allopurinal (Zyloprim) 300 mg P.O. daily.
   Available: 100-mg tablets.
   Amount to give?

3. Ordered: ampicillin 500 mg P.O. b.i.d.
   Available: 250-mg tablets.
   Amount to give?

4. Ordered: NPH insulin 22 units and regular insulin 12 units S.C.
   Available: both insulins are concentrated as 100 units/mL.
   Amount to give?

5. Ordered: cephalexin (Keflex) 1 g P.O. q.6h.
   Available: cephalexin 500-mg tablets.
   Amount to give?

6. Ordered: hydrocortisone sodium succinate (Solucortef) 100 mg I.M.
   Available: 100 mg/2 mL.
   Amount to give?

7. Ordered: levothyroxine sodium (Synthroid) 0.15 mg P.O. daily.
   Available: tablets of 0.05 mg each.
   Amount to give?

8. Ordered: meperidine (Demerol) 75 mg I.M. stat.
   Available: a 2 mL ampule of 50 mg/mL.
   Amount to give?

9. Ordered: theophylline (Theodur) 450 mg P.O. p.c.
   Available: 300-mg scored tablets.
   Amount to give?

10. Ordered: fluphenazine (Modecate) 12.5 mg I.M.
    Available: Modecate 25 mg/mL.
    Amount to give?

11. Ordered: digoxin (Lanoxin) 0.125 mg P.O.
    Available: 0.25-mg scored tablets.
    Amount to give?

12. Ordered: heparin 6 000 units.
    Available: heparin 10 000 units/mL.
    Amount to give?

Ordered: penicillin G potassium 1 000 000 units q.i.d.
Available: tablets of 500 000 units each.
Calculate the following:

13. Number of tablets to give for each dosage time

14. Number of tablets necessary for each day

15. Number of tablets required for one week's supply

For questions 16–20, indicate whether there is an error in calculation or interpretation of the medication order. You will have to read carefully to detect some of the errors.

16. Ordered: Drug New 250 mg P.O. q.i.d.
    Available: 250-mg tablets
    Give 1 mg.

17. Ordered: Drug Old 50 mg I.M. stat.
    Available: ampule labelled 50 mg/mL.
    Give 1 ampule.

18. Ordered: Drug R 50 mg I.M. p.r.n.
    Available: Drug R 50 mg/mL.
    Give 50 mL.

19. Ordered: Drug Y 100 mg t.i.d. p.c.
    Available: Drug Y 50-mg tablets.
    Give 2 tablets one half hour before meals

20. Ordered: Drug P 15 mg P.O. in three divided doses.
    Available: Drug P 2.5-mg tablets.
    Give 2 tablets each time.

# POST-TEST

## Instructions

1. Write the post-test without referring to any reference materials and without the aid of a calculator.

2. Correct the post-test using the answer guide.

3. If your score is 100 percent, proceed to the next module.

4. If you don't achieve 100 percent, review the appropriate sections of the learning package in this module and rewrite the post-test.

5. Be *careful* to include units with all answers, e.g., mg, mL, tablets. Round off decimal numbers to the nearest hundredth.

1. The order is: phenobarbital (Luminal) 0.3 g P.O. The dose on hand is in 100-mg tablets. How many tablets should you give?

2. The order is: probenecid (Benemid) 750 mg P.O. The dose on hand is 500-mg (scored) tablets. Determine the correct dosage to administer.

3. A physician orders penicillin 400 000 units I.M. The label indicates penicillin 300 000 units/mL. Determine the correct dosage to give.

4. From reserpine (Serpasil) tablets of 0.25 mg each, determine the correct dosage for an order of 0.5 mg P.O.

5. Oxytetracycline hydrochloride (Terramycin) 0.25 g is ordered I.M., and the vial is labelled: 250 mg/2mL. How many mL should you give?

6. Aspirin 0.65 g is ordered. You have tablets of 325 mg each. How many tablets should you give?

7. The physician orders 25 units of NPH insulin. The dose on hand is 100 units per mL. Determine the correct dosage.

8. The patient is to receive 800 $\mu$g of drug S. The drug is labelled: 0.4 mg per tablet. How many tablets should be given?

9. The physician's order is for heparin 2 500 units S.C. The dose on hand is available in two strengths: heparin 1 000 units per mL and heparin 10 000 units per mL. Calculate the dosage for each strength.

The order is: 35 units NPH insulin and 15 units of regular insulin. The vials indicate that each drug is available in 100 units/mL. Calculate:

10. The volume of NPH insulin required.

11. The volume of CZI insulin required.

12. The total volume that should be drawn up in one syringe (These two insulins are mixed and administered in the same syringe).

13. The physician orders 0.125 mg of digoxin (Lanoxin) P.O. daily. The drug is labelled: 0.25 mg per tablet. How many tablets would the patient require for a 14-day supply?

14. You are to give 2 000 mg of Drug B. The label indicates that each tablet is 1 g. How many tablets should you give?

The order is: 500 000 units I.V. q.6h. On hand you have a 10 mL vial that is labelled 10 000 000 units. Calculate:

15. The concentration of drug per mL.

16. The volume required to administer the dose ordered.

17. The number of dosages this vial contains (for the amount ordered for this patient).

The order is:
    morphine sulfate 10 mg I.M.
    atropine sulfate 0.4 mg I.M. one hour pre-op.

The ampules are labelled
    morphine sulfate 10 mg/mL
    atropine sulfate 0.6 mg/mL
Calculate:

18. The dosage of morphine.

19. The dosage of atropine.

20. The total volume in the syringe after the two drugs are drawn up. (These drugs can be mixed together for a short time.)

21. Your patient is learning to administer her insulin. The order is for 22 units of Ultralente insulin and 8 units of Semilente insulin. The vial for each insulin is labelled: 100 units/mL. She asks you to check her dosage. The syringe markings indicate she has drawn up 0.3 mL. Is this correct?

22. The physician orders 75-mg tablets p.r.n. for pain. The dose on hand is 50-mg scored tabs. How many tablets would you give?

23. The patient is to receive phenytoin (Dilantin pediatric) suspension 25 mg P.O. t.i.d. The bottle in the drug cabinet reads: 30 mg/5 mL. How many mL should be administered for each dose?

24. The physician has ordered penicillin G sodium (Crystapen) 600 000 units I.M. The drug label reads: 400 000 units/mL. How many mL should the patient receive?

25. The order is for bromocriptine mesylate (Parlodel) $\frac{1}{2}$ tab with breakfast and 1 tab with supper. The drug is supplied in scored 2.5 mg tablets. Calculate the total amount of drug taken daily.

YOUR SCORE: _____ %

100%      YES—proceed to next module
          NO—review this module

---

**Note:** if you had any errors on the post-test, analyze your areas of weakness here before reviewing the appropriate section of the module.

# Module 8: Solutions

## PRE-TEST

## Instructions

1. Write the pre-test without referring to any resource materials and without the aid of a calculator.

2. Correct the pre-test using the answer guide.

3. Be careful to:
   a. include the appropriate units of measurement with the answer when necessary
   b. follow directions regarding rounding numbers
   c. write decimal numbers correctly, e.g. using a zero in front of the decimal point when necessary.
   You should deduct marks if your answers aren't expressed correctly as indicated above.

4. If your score is 100 percent, proceed to the next module.

5. If you don't achieve 100 percent accuracy, read the learning package in this module and complete the exercises, concentrating on your weak areas as diagnosed by your pre-test score.

## Definitions

Define each of the following terms in your own words and according to the module definitions:

1. *solute*


2. *solution*


3. *solvent*


4. *strength or concentration*


5. The term *percent concentration* describes the strength of a solution by stating the parts of solute, or pure drug, in how many parts of solution? _____ parts.

6. A solution is labelled 5%. This means there are _____ parts of drug in _____ of solution.

7. In a volume per volume solution with 5 mL of pure drug, the solution would be measured in _____ .

8. Express the following solution strength as a ratio:
    0.9% =

For the following questions, choose the best answer:

9. A solution that has 1 g of pure drug, solute, in 2 000 mL of solution is termed a:
    a. weight per weight solution
    b. weight per volume solution
    c. volume per volume solution
    d. volume per weight solution

10. Which of the following descriptions of solution concentration describes a weight per volume solution?
    a. 5 mL in 100 mL
    b. 2 g in 150 mL
    c. 10 mg in 100 mg
    d. 25:1 000

## Conversions

Convert each of the following percent concentrations of solutions to ratio concentrations. Express your answers in whole numbers and in lowest terms.

11. 5%                          12. 0.3%

13. 3.3%                        14. 60%

15. 10%                         16. 0.9%

Convert each of the following ratio concentrations of solutions to a percent concentration. Express your answers in decimal numbers rounded to the nearest tenth.

17. 1:20                        18. 5:1

19. 1:1 000                     20. 1:4

21. 1:10 000

## Calculations

For each of the following solution concentrations, calculate the amount of solute, pure drug, that is dissolved in the solution. Express your answers in decimal numbers rounded to the nearest tenth. Include the appropriate unit of measurement with your answers.

22. How many g of sodium chloride are in 1 L of a 0.9% solution?

23. How many g of dextrose are in 500 mL of a 5% solution?

24. How many mg of epinephrine are in 1 mL of a 1:1 000 solution?

For each of the following solutions, calculate the percent and the ratio strengths of the solution. State percent concentrations rounded to the nearest tenth. State ratio concentrations in whole numbers.

| Solution | Ratio Concentration | Percent Concentration |
|---|---|---|
| 25.  2 g drug in 1 L | _____ | _____ |
| 26.  500 mg drug in 30 mL | _____ | _____ |
| 27.  0.5 g of drug in 100 mL | _____ | _____ |
| 28.  20 mL of drug in 1 000 mL | _____ | _____ |
| 29.  1 g of drug in 2 mL | _____ | _____ |
| 30.  1 mg of drug in 1 mL | _____ | _____ |

YOUR SCORE: _____ %

100%    YES—proceed to the next module
NO—complete this module

**Note:** If you had any errors on the pre-test, analyze your areas of weakness here.

## Learning Package

### Objective 8

**To convert solutions expressed as ratio and percent concentration; to calculate the amount of pure drug in solutions; to calculate percent or ratio strengths of solutions**

### Definitions

A **solution** is a homogeneous mixture that contains one or more dissolved substances in a liquid. For example, when you add sugar to your tea you are creating a solution.

A **solvent** is the liquid in which another substance is dissolved. In the above example, the tea is the solvent.

A **solute** is the substance dissolved in the solvent. In our example, sugar is a solute.

Some drugs are available in solution; the drug is the solute, and water is usually the solvent. In other instances, normal saline, alcohol, or other liquids are used as solvents.

When drugs are prepared in solution, they are described by the **strength** or **concentration** of the solution.

The strength or concentration of a solution is determined by the amount of solute dissolved in a given amount of solvent. For example, did you put one teaspoon or two teaspoons of sugar in your cup of tea?

An example of strength of solutions is demonstrated by the preparation of heparin. This is done in varying strengths, such as 1 000 units per mL and 10 000 units per mL. The latter preparation is ten times greater in concentration than the former.

## Exercise 8.1

Complete the following exercise without referring to the previous text. Correct using the answer guide.

Complete each of the following sentences with the most appropriate term.

1. A homogeneous mixture that contains one or more dissolved substances in a liquid is called a _____ .

2. The substance that is dissolved in a solution is called a _____ .

3. In a solution, the liquid in which a substance is dissolved is called a _____ .

Read the description of this drug and then answer questions 4 and 5.

> Add 4.6 mL of sterile water to obtain
> penicillin G potassium 200 000 units per mL.

4. In this drug solution, name the solute:

5. In this drug solution, name the solvent:

Indicate whether the following sentence is true or false:

6. The strength or concentration of a solution is determined by the amount of solute dissolved in a given amount of solvent.

For the following questions, choose the best answer:

7. Which solution has the greater concentration?
   a. 1 000 units per 1 mL
   b. 10 000 units per 1 mL

8. The labels on two vials of the same medication indicate that the concentrations are:
   Drug A: 10 mg/mL
   Drug B: 100 mg in 10 mL

   Is the concentration of Drug A:
   a. the same as Drug B
   b. less than Drug B
   c. greater than Drug B?

## Types of Solutions

There are many types of solutions and, in most instances involving drugs, they are pre-mixed. The two types of solutions that are relevant in medication therapy are illustrated in Figure 8.1 and explained further.

1. A weight per volume solution: the solute is weighed, but the solvent is expressed in volume: grams to millilitres.

Most intravenous solutions are expressed as a weight per volume type of solution: a given weight of dextrose, in g, is dissolved in a certain volume of water, in mL.

Comparing unlike units of measurements is acceptable in this situation because of the following principle:

> 1 mL of distilled water, at 4 degrees C, weighs 1 g. Therefore,
> 1 mL of water could be considered equal to 1 g.

This is important to remember later when you begin calculating dosages involving solutions. For the purpose of these calculations, g and mL can be used if they were equivalent units of measurement.

2. A volume per volume solution: both the solute and the solvent are measured in the same units of volume. For example, 1 mL of drug may be dissolved in 10 mL of water or alcohol.

The label indicates whether the solution is a weight per volume (w/v) or volume per volume (v/v) type of solution by giving the units of measurement of the solute and the solvent.

> e.g., 1 tsp in 1 fluid oz is a volume per volume
> e.g., 1 g per 100 mL is a weight per volume

The most frequent type you will encounter is the weight per volume solution. The solute is the pure drug that is weighed in g, and the solvent, usually distilled sterile water, is measured by volume, in mL. Remember this: it is grams to millilitres!

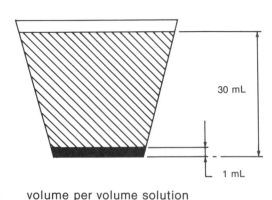

weight per volume solution            volume per volume solution

**Figure 8.1**  Types of solutions

## Exercise 8.2

Complete the following exercise without referring to the previous text. Correct using the answer guide.

Complete questions 1 to 4 by indicating the unit of measurement for the solute and the solvent for each type of solution. Choose your response from this list of units: gram, milligram, millilitre.

1. In a weight per volume solution, the unit of measurement of the solute is a _____ .

2. In a weight per volume solution, the unit of measurement of the solvent is a _____ .

3. In a volume per volume solution, the unit of measurement of the solute is a _____ .

4. In a volume per volume solution, the unit of measurement of the solvent is a _____ .

Indicate whether the following solutions are weight per volume or volume per volume type:

5. A solution that has 5 g of solute, pure drug, dissolved in 100 mL of solvent is termed a _____ solution.

6. You have mixed 5 mL of lemon juice with 250 mL of water. You have prepared a _____ type of solution.

## Percent and Ratio Concentration

The strength or concentration of a solution is expressed as a *percent concentration* or *ratio concentration*.

The term percent means "parts in a hundred." A percent strength describes how many parts of drug are found in 100 parts of solution. For example, a 5% solution has 5 parts of drug, or solute, dissolved in 100 parts of solution.

Of course, these parts must be equivalent. In a volume per volume solution, both the drug and the solution are measured by volume, such as mL. In a weight per volume solution, the drug is measured in grams, and the solvent is measured in millilitres. For example, a 1% weight per volume solution has 1 g dissolved in 100 mL solution.

A ratio is a comparable expression of solution strength but does not necessarily use 100 as the measurement base. For example, the ratio 1:10 means there is 1 part of the drug, or solute, dissolved in 10 parts of solution. Similarily, 1:1 000 indicates that in a solution of 1 000 parts, only 1 part is drug.

## Exercise 8.3

Complete the following questions without referring to the previous text. Correct using the answer guide.

1. In relation to a solution, explain the term *percent concentration*.

2. In relation to a solution, explain the term *ratio concentration*.

3. In a particular drug product there are 2 parts of solute, or drug, and 10 parts of solution. Express this as a ratio concentration:

Complete the following sentence:

4. A 15% solution means there are _____ parts of solute, or drug, in _____ parts of solution.

## Converting Ratio and Percent Solutions

When calculating drug dosages, it is necessary to express the strength of the required dose in the same manner as the strength of the available dose. The medication order may ask for a 1% solution, and the label may indicate that the drug concentration is 1:100. You need to know the relationship between percent and ratio to determine whether you have the correct drug concentration. Recall Module 4: Ratio and Proportion.

### Converting a Ratio to a Percent Concentration

1. Express the ratio as a fraction:
$$1:100 = \frac{1}{100}$$
2. Multiply by 100
$$\frac{1}{100} \times 100 = 1$$
3. Add the % sign
$$1\%$$

Conclusion: a ratio strength of 1:100 means that there is 1 part drug in 100 parts of solution, and this is equal to a 1% solution.

Examples:
$$4:5 = \frac{4}{5} = \frac{4}{5} \times 100 = 80\%$$
$$3:2 = \frac{3}{2} = \frac{3}{2} \times 100 = 150\%$$
$$1:1\ 000 = \frac{1}{1\ 000} = \frac{1}{1\ 000} \times 100 = 0.1\%$$

### Converting Percent to a Ratio Concentration

1. Place the percent value over 100:

   $0.9\% = \frac{0.9}{100}$

2. Express the fraction using whole numbers:

   $\frac{0.9}{100} = \frac{9}{1\,000}$

3. Reduce the fraction to its lowest term:

   $\frac{9}{1\,000}$

4. Express as a ratio by placing the numerator first and the denominator second:

   $\frac{9}{1\,000} = 9{:}1\,000$

Conclusion: a percent strength of 0.9% means that there are 0.9 parts of drug per 100 parts of solution, or 9 parts of drug per 1 000 parts of solution, and this is equal to a ratio solution of 9:1 000.

---

Examples:

$5\% = \frac{5}{100} = \frac{1}{20} = 1{:}20$

$3.3\% = \frac{3.3}{100} = \frac{33}{1\,000} = 33{:}1\,000$

$10\% = \frac{10}{100} \text{ (reduced)} = \frac{1}{10} = 1{:}10$

---

## Exercise 8.4

Complete the following exercise without referring to the previous text and without the aid of a calculator. Correct using the answer guide.

Convert each of the following ratio concentrations to percent concentrations. Express your answer in decimal numbers rounded to the nearest tenth.

1. 1:25
2. 1:1 000
3. 1:10 000
4. 0.075:1
5. 1:1

Convert each of the following percent concentrations to ratio concentrations. Express your answer in whole numbers.

6. 10%
7. 0.45%
8. 25%
9. 3.3%
10. 5%

## Calculations Involving Solutions

Many medications administered daily in the home and in institutions are prepared as solutions. When you give a pre-med of morphine, you inject a solution that has a specified amount of morphine dissolved in each mL of solution. Fortunately, the label usually indicates this concentration; e.g., 10 mg/mL. Because the drug order specifies the amount of drug by weight, such as 10 mg morphine, this calculation is a simple one.

Sometimes the calculations are more complex. If the physician orders 1 mL of epinephrine 1:1 000, how much drug is the patient receiving?

To answer this question, we must determine the amount of solute, or pure drug, dissolved in the solution. This can be done by multiplying the volume of the solution by the strength of the solution.

> solute = strength × volume of solution
> OR
> amount of pure drug = strength × volume

### Explanation of Measurements

The *amount of pure drug* is expressed in g or mL, depending on whether it is a weight per volume or volume per volume solution.
The strength of the solution is written as a fraction.
The volume of the solution is expressed in mL.

---

Example:

How many mg of epinephrine are in 1 mL of a 1:1 000 solution of epinephrine?
1. Amount of pure drug = ? g
2. Strength = 1:1 000 or $\frac{1}{1\,000}$
3. Volume of solution = 1 mL
4. Type of solution: weight per volume solution, and this means the drug, or solute, is measured in g and the solvent is measured in mL.
5. State the formula:

   amount of pure drug = strength × volume of solution
6. Substitute the values into the formula and calculate:
   $? = \frac{1}{1\,000} \times 1$

   $? = \frac{1}{1\,000}$ g or 0.001 g

The question asks for the amount of drug in mg.
Convert the answer to mg.
Recall that 1 g = 1 000 mg.
Therefore 0.001 g = 1 mg.
The patient received 1 mg of epinephrine.

Let's try another common example. How many g of dextrose are contained in 1 L of a 5% intravenous fluid? You may want to know this to calculate the kilojoules your patient receives with each L of I.V. Each g of dextrose supplies 11.3 kilojoules or 3.4 K calories.

1. Amount of drug (dextrose) = n
2. Strength = 5% or $\frac{5}{100}$
3. Volume of solution = 1 L or 1 000 L
4. Type of solution: weight per volume; therefore, the drug is measured in g.
5. State the formula:

   amount of drug = strength × volume of solution

6. Analyze this problem and substitute the given values into the formula, then calculate:

   n = $\frac{5}{100}$ × 1 000

   n = 50 g

For every L of 5% dextrose in water, the patient receives 50 g of dextrose. This would, therefore, supply 565 kilojoules, or 170 kilocalories.

A final example: a frequently used I.V. solution contains 3.3% dextrose and 0.3% saline. (An imaginative individual nicknamed this the $\frac{2}{3}:\frac{1}{3}$ solution!) Calculate:

a. the amount of dextrose in 1 L
b. the amount of sodium chloride in 1 L

a. n = $\frac{33}{1\,000}$ × 1 000

   n = 33 g of dextrose

b. n = $\frac{3}{1\,000}$ × 1 000

   n = 3 g of NaCl

## Exercise 8.5

Complete the following exercise without referring to the previous text and without the aid of a calculator. Correct using the answer guide.

1. The label indicates: epinephrine 1:1 000. If you administer 0.1 mL of this solution, how many mg of epinephrine will the patient receive?

2. The physician's order for a child states: "give epinephrine 10 $\mu$g S.C. stat." How many mL should be administered from a vial that contains epinephrine 1:1 000?

3. The order is for 0.5 mL of a 1:1 000 solution. If the nurse uses a vial labelled: 1:10 000 and draws up 0.5 mL, what is the error in dosage?

4. How many g of dextrose are in 500 mL of a 5% solution?

5. How many g of salt are needed to prepare a L of a 0.9% solution?

## Calculating Strengths of Solutions

Some clinical situations require that you convert the desired dosage and the available dosage to the same expressions of strength or concentration. This can be achieved by several mathematical approaches. Two methods are described here.

First Method: describe the ratio concentration of the solute to solution by stating the mL or g of the drug in mL of solution.

> Example:  5 000 mg of drug per L
>                 5 g per 1 000 mL
>                 5:1 000 or 1:200
> Convert the ratio to a percent,
> as learned previously in this module:
> $$1:200 = \frac{1}{200} \times 100 = 0.5\%$$

Second Method:  use formula number 1 to solve for the concentration expressed as a fraction:

amount of pure drug = strength × volume of solution

> Example:  5 000 mg of drug per L
> $$5 \text{ g} = \frac{?}{100} \times 1\ 000 \text{ mL}$$
> $$? = 0.5$$
> Convert the fraction to a ratio or percent:
> percent: $\frac{0.5}{100} = 0.5\%$
> ratio: $\frac{0.5}{100} = 0.5:100$ or 5:1 000 or 1:200

## Exercise 8.6

Complete the following exercise without referring to the previous text and without the aid of a calculator. Correct using the answer guide.

For each of the following solutions, calculate the percent or the ratio strengths of the solution. State percent concentrations rounded to the nearest tenth. State ratio concentrations in whole numbers.

1. What percent is a solution that has 50 g of solute, pure drug, in 1 L?

2. What is the ratio strength of a solution that has 1 mg of drug in 1 mL of solution?

3. What is the percent strength of a solution of 250 mg per mL?

4. Epinephrine 1:1 000 solution for injection contains how much drug, i.e., epinephrine?

   a. 1 mg per ampule
   b. 1 µg per mL
   c. 1 mg per mL
   d. 1 g per mL

# POST-TEST

## Instructions

1. Write the post-test without referring to any resources and without the aid of a calculator.

2. Correct using the answer guide.

3. Be careful to:
   a. include the appropriate units of measurement with the answer when necessary
   b. follow directions regarding rounding numbers
   c. write decimal numbers correctly, using a zero in front of the decimal point when necessary.
   You should deduct marks if your answers aren't expressed correctly, as indicated above.

4. If you achieve 100 percent, you have completed the modules required for dosage calculations in most clinical settings, assuming that you proceeded through the modules in sequence. Congratulations!

Modules 9 and 10 prepare you for specific skill involving intravenous medications and fractional dosages encountered in pediatric and specialized practice settings.

5. If you don't achieve 100 percent, review the learning package in this module and re-write the post-test. You may wish to seek further assistance through the references listed in the bibliography.

## Conversions:

Convert each of the following percent concentrations of solutions to ratio concentrations. Express your answers in whole numbers.

| | |
|---|---|
| 1. 5% | 2. 0.3% |
| 3. 3.3% | 4. 60% |
| 5. 10% | 6. 0.9% |

Convert each of the following ratio concentrations of solutions to percent concentrations. Express your answers in decimal numbers rounded to the nearest tenth.

| | |
|---|---|
| 7. 1:20 | 8. 5:1 |
| 9. 1:1 000 | 10. 1:4 |
| 11. 1:10 000 | |

## Calculations:

For each of the following solution concentrations, calculate the amount of solute, pure drug, that is dissolved in the solution. Express your answers in decimal numbers rounded to the nearest tenth. Include the appropriate unit of measurement with each answer.

12. How many g of sodium chloride are in 1 L of a 0.9% solution?

13. How many g of dextrose are in 500 mL of a 5% solution?

14. How many mg of epinephrine are in 1 mL of a 1:1 000 solution?

For each of the following solutions, calculate the percent and the ratio strengths of the solution. State percent concentrations rounded to the nearest tenth. State ratio concentrations in whole numbers.

|  | Ratio Concentration | Percent Concentration |
|---|---|---|
| 15. 1 g drug in 1 L | _____ | _____ |
| 16. 50 mg drug in 50 mL | _____ | _____ |
| 17. 0.5 g of drug in 10 mL | _____ | _____ |
| 18. 250 mL of drug in 1 000 mL | _____ | _____ |
| 19. 1 g of drug in 2 mL | _____ | _____ |
| 20. 15 mg of drug in 1 mL | _____ | _____ |

## Definitions:

Define each of the following terms in your own words and according to the module definitions.

21. *solute*                     22. *solution*

23. *solvent*                    24. *strength* or *concentration*

Complete the following sentences with the most appropriate term or terms:

25. The term *percent concentration* describes the strength of a solution by stating the parts of solute, or pure drug, in how many parts of solution? _____ parts.

26. In a weight per volume solution, the unit of measurement of the solute is _____, and the unit of measurement of the solvent is _____.

27. In a volume per volume solution with 5 mL of pure drug, the solution would be measured in _____.

28. The expression that there are 5 parts of solute, or pure drug, dissolved in 20 parts of solution is termed a _____ (*ratio* or *percent*) *concentration*?

For the following questions, choose the best answer:

29. A solution that has 1 g of pure drug, solute, in 2 000 mL of solution is termed a:

    a. weight per weight solution

    b. weight per volume solution

    c. volume per volume solution

    d. volume per weight solution

30. Which of the following descriptions of solution concentration describes a weight per volume solution?

    a.  5 mL in 100 mL

    b.  2 g in 150 mL

    c.  10 mg in 100 mg

    d.  25:1 000

YOUR SCORE: _____ %

100%      YES—proceed to the next module
             NO—review this module

---

**Note:** if you had any errors on the post-test, analyze your areas of weakness here before reviewing the appropriate section of this module.

# Module 9: Intravenous Medications

## PRE-TEST

### Instructions

1. Write the pre-test without referring to any resource materials and without the aid of a calculator.

2. Correct the pre-test using the answer guide.

3. Be careful to:
   a. include the appropriate units of measurement with the answer when necessary
   b. round decimals to nearest whole number
   c. write decimal numbers correctly, using a zero in front of the decimal point when necessary.

   You should deduct marks if your answers aren't expressed correctly, as indicated above.

4. If your score is 100 percent, you are ready for the "real world" of calculating most medications for administration to patients in the clinical setting—assuming, of course, that you have mastered the preceding modules.

5. If you don't achieve 100 percent accuracy, read the learning package in this module and complete the exercises, concentrating on your weak areas as diagnosed by your pre-test score.

For each of the following clinical situations, calculate as directed:

Order 1: the patient is to receive 1 L of I.V. fluid in 8 hours.

1. For order 1, calculate the number of mL per minute that the patient should receive.

2. For order 1, calculate the rate of flow in drops per minute (drop factor is 10).

3. A 500 mL I.V. is infusing at the rate of 30 mL per hour. How many hours will it take for this I.V. to be infused?

Order 2: 1 L q.12h.

4. For order 2, calculate the volume to be infused in one hour.

5. For order 2, calculate the rate of flow using a minidrip set (drop factor is 60).

6. Ampicillin has been added to 50 mL of normal saline. The drug should be infused in 20 minutes. Calculate the rate of flow using a regular set with a drop factor of 1 mL = 10 drops.

Order 3: 2 L per day.

7. For order 3, calculate the hourly rate of infusion.

8. For order 3, calculate the drip rate (drop factor is 60).

9. The order is for 1 500 mL of saline over 24 hours. Calculate the infusion rate per minute if the administration set delivers 10 drops per mL.

10. A L of I.V. fluid has been running at 125 mL per hour for 3.5 hours. How much is remaining in the I.V. container?

11. The I.V. is ordered to run at 50 mL per hour. The administration set delivers 60 drops per mL. Calculate the infusion rate in drops per minute.

12. The I.V. container is labelled: "infuse at 100 mL per hour." The administration set delivers 10 drops per mL. The I.V. is running at a rate of 20 drops per minute. Is this correct?

13. An I.V. container of 500 mL has infused for 1 hour at a rate of 100 mL per hour. A new rate of infusion is ordered at 50 mL per hour. Calculate the number of hours during which the remaining fluid will infuse.

14. The order is for 500 mL of blood over 3 hours. Calculate the rate of flow using a set with a drop factor of 15.

15. The I.V. is infusing at 125 drops per minute with a minidrip (drop factor is 60). How long will it take to infuse 250 mL?


YOUR SCORE: _____ %

100%      YES—proceed to the next module
          NO—complete this module

---

**Note:** if you had any errors on the pre-test, analyze your areas of weakness here.

## Learning Package

### Objective 9

**To accurately calculate the rate of flow of intravenous infusions using various drop factors**

## Calculating Rate of Flow of Intravenous Infusions

All intravenous fluids and medications must be administered precisely. The desired rate of flow must be calculated accurately and observed frequently during intravenous therapy.

The volume and type of intravenous fluid is ordered by the physician. The safe rate of administration of I.V. fluids and medications is determined by many factors, including:

1. Age. Infants and the elderly tolerate less fluid.

2. Cardiovascular status.

3. Site of infusion.

4. Nature of the infusion, e.g., irritating fluids or medications must be infused slowly to allow for adequate hemodilution.

5. B.S.A., body surface area: the maximum rate of flow should not exceed 3 mL per square metre.

Intravenous fluids are administered either by infusion pumps or by gravity drip. When a pump is used the rate of flow is expressed in mL per hour. For gravity drip, the rate must be calculated in drops per minute. This requires an additional step in the calculation. This module focuses on clinical situations involving gravity drip.

To calculate the rate of flow for a gravity drip, you must know the following:

1. The ordered rate of flow which must be converted to drops per minute in order to regulate the intravenous administration set.

2. The calibration of the administration set in drops per mL. Different sets are unique in this factor.

To calculate the rate of flow, use this formula:

$$\frac{\text{volume of fluid (mL)}}{\text{time to infuse (minutes)}} \times \frac{\text{calibration}}{\text{of I.V.set}}$$

Example: the order is 5% dextrose, 1 L q.8h.
using a regular set; drop factor = 10

Step 1. Volume of fluid in mL = 1 000

Step 2. Time to infuse in minutes = 8 × 60 = 480

Step 3. Calibration of I.V. set: refers to the number
of drops in each mL. Determined by the
I.V. set. Labelled on the I.V. tubing box.
In this example, we are using a regular set
with a drop factor of 10. This means that
it requires 10 drops from the drip chamber
to deliver 1 mL.

Calculate:

$$\frac{1\ 000}{8 \times 60} \times 10 = 21 \text{ drops per minute}$$
approximately

Now it is possible to time the drops from the I.V. drip chamber and regulate this I.V. to infuse over 8 hours.

Not all I.V. sets deliver the same size of drops. It is essential that you determine the type of drip chamber being used. A minidrip delivers approximately 60 drops per mL. The calculated rate of flow would differ considerably from the one above. However, the actual volume the patient receives would remain the same.

Example: calculate the above using a minidrip

$$\frac{1\ 000}{8 \times 60} \times 60 = 125 \text{ drops/min}$$

## Exercise 9.1

Complete the following exercise without referring to the previous text and without the aid of a calculator. Correct using the answer guide.

1. Order: 1 L of normal saline q.12h. Calculate the rate of flow using a minidrip with a drop factor of 60 drops per mL.

2. Order: 1 000 mL of two-thirds/one-third to run at 50 drops per minute. How many hours should this litre infuse using a minidrip (drop factor is 60)?

Order: 3 000 mL of 5% dextrose over 24 hours.

3. For this order, calculate the rate of flow using a regular set (drop factor is 10).

4. For this order, calculate the rate of flow using a minidrip set (drop factor is 60).

5. The blood transfusion is infusing at 25 drops per minute, and the set is calibrated at 15 drops per mL. What is the hourly infusion rate, in mL?

Order: administer 3 000 mL/sq m × 24 hours. The patient's body surface area is 1.21 square meters. (The concept of body surface area is discussed in Module 10 but the arithmetic principles should be clear to you).

6. For this order, calculate the total amount of fluid to infuse in 24 hours.

7. For this order, calculate the hourly infusion rate.

8. For this order, calculate the rate in drops per minute using a regular drip infusion set (drop factor is 10).

9. The ordered dose of methotrexate is dissolved in 1 L to be infused over 1 hour. Calculate the rate of flow in drops/min using a regular drip set (drop factor is 10).

10. The order is to infuse 1.5 litres of N/S (normal saline) with an antineoplastic drug, over 6 hours. Using a regular drip, drop factor of 10, calculate the rate of flow.

# POST-TEST

## Instructions

1. Write the post-test without referring to any reference materials and without the aid of a calculator.

2. Correct the post-test using the answer guide.

3. Be careful to:

   a. include the appropriate units of measurement with the answer when necessary

   b. round decimals to nearest whole number

   c. write decimal numbers correctly, using a zero in front of the decimal point when necessary

   You should deduct marks if your answers are not expressed correctly, as indicated above.

4. If your score is 100 percent, congratulations! You are ready for the "real world" of calculating most medications for administration to patients in the clinical setting—assuming, of course, that you have mastered the preceding modules. Module 10 explains more complex but less common clinical calculations. You will want to proceed to this module before practicing in the following settings: pediatrics, coronary or extra care units, emergency, and neonatal units.

5. If you don't achieve 100 percent, review the learning package in this module and rewrite the post-test. You may wish to seek further assistance through the references listed in the bibliography.

For each of the following clinical situations, calculate as directed:

Order 1: 1 000 mL q.8h.

1. For order 1, calculate the rate of flow using a minidrip (drop factor is 60).

2. For order 1, calculate the rate of flow using a set with a drop factor of 10.

Order 2: aminophylline 50 mg per hour, to be given by continuous infusion. The intravenous manual instructions are: "dilute to a concentration of 1 mg/mL of dextrose or normal saline."

3. For order 2, calculate the volume of fluid required for a 2-hour infusion.

4. For order 2, calculate the rate of flow using a minidrip set (drop factor is 60).

5. For order 2, a 50 mL minibag is marked: "contains 50 mg of aminophylline." It is infusing at 50 drops per minute (drop factor is 60). How much drug is infused in 30 minutes?

6. For order 2, calculate the length of time to infuse this drug if 500 mg is added to 500 mL and a minidrip set is used (drop factor is 60).

Order 3: ampicillin 250 mg q.6h. The patient has an I.V. infusing with a minidrip set (drop factor is 60). The intravenous manual instructions are: "dilute to 5 mg/mL and infuse over 30 minutes."

7. For order 3, calculate the volume of fluid required to dilute the drug.

8. For order 3, calculate the rate of flow.

Order 4: 1 000 mL q.8h. × 24 hours. After 3 hours, with a regular set (drop factor is 10), only 300 mL are absorbed.

9. For order 4, calculate the volume that should have infused in the 3-hour time period.

10. For order 4, calculate the new rate of flow for the remaining 700 mL to be absorbed within the ordered time period.

11. Calculate the rate of flow (drop factor is 10) for this order: "500 mL over 3 hours."

12. Using an administration set with a drop factor of 15 and an infusion rate of 15 drops per minute, how long would be required to infuse 60 mL?

13. A 100-mL minibag infusing at 50 drops per minute (drop factor is 60) is initiated at 1000 hours. At what time should it be completely infused?

14. An I.V. is infusing at 125 mL per hour. How many mL will be absorbed in a 12-hour shift?

15. An I.V. infuses at 20 drops per minute (drop factor is 10) for 4 hours. How much has infused?

YOUR SCORE: _____ %

100%    YES—proceed to the next module
        NO—review this module

**Note:** if you had any errors on the post-test, analyze your areas of weakness here before reviewing the appropriate section of the module.

# Module 10: Fractional Dosages

## PRE-TEST

### Instructions

1. Write the pre-test without referring to any resources and without the aid of a calculator.

2. Express all decimal numbers rounded to the nearest hundredth.

3. Correct the pre-test using the answer guide.

4. If your score is 100 percent, congratuations! You have finished the workbook, assuming that you proceeded through the modules in sequence.

5. If you don't achieve 100 percent accuracy, read the learning package in this module and complete the exercises, concentrating on your weak areas as diagnosed by your pre-test score.

**Note:** this module is designed to test advanced skills in dosage calculation. Don't proceed if you are faint-hearted. If you do proceed, don't be discouraged if you diagnose weaknesses in your ability to calculate intravenous administration of medications. This is a very challenging area, as any health professional in an acute care setting will agree.

1. Calculate the dose to be administered:
    ordered: 5 mg/kg P.O.
    available: 250 mg tablets
    patient weighs 50 kg

2. Calculate the dose to be administered:
    ordered: 10 $\mu$g/kg epinephrine S.C. stat
    available: epinephrine 1:1 000
    child weighs 10 kg

Order 1: Drug B 25 mg/kg P.O. daily in 3 divided doses.

3. For order 1, calculate *each* dose for a patient weighing 60 kg.

4. For order 1, calculate the dosage in tablets if available strength is 250 mg tablets.

5. An antibiotic is ordered: 2 g per square metre (body surface area). A child's B.S.A. is 0.45 sq m. Calculate the dose to administer.

**Note:** a child's dose is calculated with the formula:

$$\text{child's dose} = \frac{\text{B.S.A.}}{1.73 \text{ sq m}} \times \text{adult dose}$$

6. Using the formula: if the usual adult dose is 60 mg, calculate the dose for a child with a B.S.A. of 0.2 sq m.

121

7. Using the formula: if the usual adult dose is 250 mg, calculate the dose for a child with a B.S.A. of 1 sq m.

8. Using the formula: if the usual adult dose is 50 mg, calculate the dose for a child with a B.S.A. of 0.86 sq m.

9. Calculate the rate of infusion in drops per minute for this order: dopamine (Intropin) 3 $\mu$g/kg/min for a patient weighing 70 kg. Use a minibag containing 200 mg dopamine in 250 mL and a minidrip infusion set (drop factor of 60 drops per mL).

Order 2: give 2 $\mu$g/kg/min I.V.

10. For order 2, calculate the dosage required for a patient weighing 65 kg.

11. For order 2, calculate the drug concentration in $\mu$g/mL if 200 mg of drug is added to 250 mL of I.V. fluid.

12. For order 2, calculate the rate of flow in drops per minute using a minidrip infusion set (drop factor is 60) and the drug concentration in question 11.

13. An I.V. minibag admixture is prepared with 1 mg of isoproterenol (Isuprel) in 250 mL of solution. Calculate the number of $\mu$g per mL.

14. The drug is ordered as 5 mg per sq m. What is the dose for an individual with a B.S.A. of 1.3 sq m?

15. If 50 mg of a drug is added to 250 mL of I.V. solution, how much drug does the patient receive per minute at a rate of 60 drops per minute (drop factor is 60).

YOUR SCORE: _____ %

100%     YES—Bravo! You have excellent skill in calculating dosages
NO—complete this module

**Note:** if you had any errors on the pre-test, analyze your areas of weakness here.

# Learning Package

> ## Objective 10
> **To accurately calculate fractional dosages based on body weight or body surface area (B.S.A.)**

In every clinical situation involving medication administration, accurate dosage calculation is an important responsibility. However, in some situations it is essential to patient safety. Neonates, pediatric, elderly, or acutely-ill patients require very precise dosage administration.

This module doesn't present any new mathematical principles but provides practice in more complex dosage calculations, using body weight, body surface area, and dosages delivered by the I.V. route.

## Calculating Dosages for Children

There are several "rules" that have been used in the past to calculate pediatric drug dosages. These rules are described in Appendix A. They were based on the child's age and the "average" adult dose. Today many references indicate the recommended dosages for children. If these aren't known, it is recognized practice to calculate pediatric dosages based on body weight or body surface area, because of the now accepted truth that children are not just "small adults." Therefore this module, in keeping with modern practice, will not discuss the old rules but will provide practice in calculating dosages based on body weight and body surface area.

## Calculations Based on Body Weight

The formula described in Module 7 applies to this situation. However, the "desired dose" must first be calculated for each patient based on body weight.

> Example:
> The order states: "give 10 mg/kg I.V. q.6h."
> The available dosage strength is: 100 mg/mL.
>
> Calculate the dosage for each of the following:
> a. A child weighing 20 kg
> b. An adult weighing 72 kg
> c. An adult weighing 61 kg
>
> The dose desired for each patient is:
> a. 10 mg × 20 kg = 200 mg
> b. 10 mg × 72 kg = 720 mg
> c. 10 mg × 61 kg = 610 mg

Now the formula can be used to determine the amount to administer.

Recall the formula:

$$\frac{\text{dose desired}}{\text{dose on hand}} \times \text{volume} = \text{volume to administer}$$

Calculate the dose to be administered to patients a and b:

a. $\frac{200}{100} \times 1 = 2$ mL. The child should receive
2 mL (via the intravenous; the actual procedure
for mixing the medication is beyond the scope
of this module).

b. $\frac{720}{100} \times 1 = 7.2$ mL. This adult should
receive 7.2 mL into the I.V.

Alternatively, ratio and proportion can also be utilized to solve the calculation problem. Let's use it to solve the calculation for the third person described in the previous example.

We know that the patient requires 610 mg and that the drug concentration is 100 mg/mL.

Therefore: $\dfrac{100 \text{ mg}}{1 \text{ ml}} = \dfrac{610 \text{ mg}}{? \text{ mL}}$

? mL = 6.1

Administer: 6.1 mL

Another example is given to illustrate dosage calculations based on body weight. In this case, the desired dose and the dose on hand are expressed in different units.

To interpret this example, you must recall some information from Module 8. Remember that a weight per volume solution describes the relationship of g to mL. In the example, epinephrine is a weight per volume solution; that is, 1 g of drug is dissolved in 1 000 mL of solvent. Therefore, this may also be expressed as 1 000 mg per 1 000 mL or 1 mg per mL.

---

Example:

The order is: 10 μg/kg epinephrine S.C. stat.
Available: epinephrine 1:1 000 = 1 mg/mL
The child weighs 15 kg.

Step 1:
Calculate the desired dose in μg (micrograms).
10 μg × 15 kg = 150 μg

Step 2:
Convert the desired dose to mg:
1 000 μg = 1 mg
150 μg = 0.15 mg
OR convert the dose on hand to μg!

Step 3:
Calculate the dosage required, in mL.

$$\frac{\text{dose desired}}{\text{dose on hand}} \times \text{volume} = \text{volume to give in mL}$$

0.15 mg/1 mg × 1 mL = 0.15 mL
Using an accurately graduated syringe, such as a
tuberculin syringe, administer 0.15 mL of
epinephrine S.C.

---

If you are confused, pause and review before doing the exercise. You could also solve the above problem using ratio and proportion. If you do that, it will help you to check the answer.

## Exercise 10.1

Complete the following exercise without referring to the previous text and without the aid of a calculator. Express all decimal numbers rounded to the nearest hundredth. Correct using the answer guide.

1. A child weighing 17 kg is to receive 5 mg/kg P.O. of an antibiotic. Available: a syrup labelled 25 mg per mL.

2. A child weighing 11.5 kg is to receive a stat dose of streptomycin sulfate 20 mg per kg I.M. Available: 250 mg per mL.

3. The order states: 0.015 mg per kg loading dose of digoxin (Lanoxin). Calculate for a child weighing 4.5 kg if available strength is 0.25 mg per mL.

4. Would you question this pre-op order for a 10-year-old boy who weighs 34 kg: atropine sulfate 0.01 mg/kg I.M. 1 h pre-op. The literature states that a maximum dose of 0.4 mg may be given to a child.

5. The order states: Drug A 20 mg/kg P.O. daily in 4 divided doses. Calculate *each* dose for a patient weighing 50 kg.

## Calculations Based on Body Surface Area

Body surface area can be used to determine the recommended doses for pediatric patients and in cancer chemotherapy. B.S.A. is calculated, using a nomogram, on the patient's height and weight. There are several such instruments available. B.S.A. correlates with several important physiological factors affecting drug dosage: blood volume, basal metabolic rate, cardiac output, and glomerular filtration.

Calculations for children based on B.S.A. involve two steps: First, calculate the body surface area using a nomogram. A schematic representation of a nomogram is illustrated in Table 10–A.

Second, calculate the dose to administer using the formula:

$$\frac{\text{child's B.S.A.}}{1.73 \text{ sq m}} \times \text{adult dose} = \text{child's dose}$$

**TABLE 10–A:**  West Nomogram for Calculating Body Surface Area

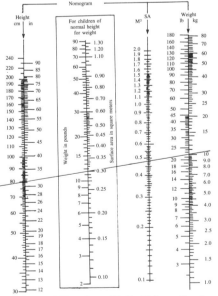

From Behrman R.E. and Vaughan, V.C. Nelson Textbook of Pediatrics, 12th edition. Philadelphia, W.B. Saunders Co. 1983. Reprinted by permission.

Example: Calculate the child's dose of Drug A, if the usual adult dose is 50 mg and the child's weight is 10 kg and height is 80 cm.

From the nomogram in Table 10–A, we determine that the child's B.S.A. is 0.48

Using the formula:

$$\frac{0.48 \text{ sq m}}{1.73 \text{ sq m}} \times 50 \text{ mg} = 13.87 \text{ mg}$$

Some drugs, such as antineoplastics for cancer treatment, are ordered for children and adults according to B.S.A. In these situations no special formula is required, just a routine calculation procedure that you have already mastered.

Example: doxorubicin (Adriamycin) 50 mg/m² I.V. today. Patient's B.S.A. is 1.21
Therefore, dose desired is
50 mg × 1.21 = 60.5 mg

## Exercise 10.2

Complete the following exercise without referring to the previous text and without the aid of a calculator. Correct using the answer guide.

1. Prescriber orders 600 mg per sq m I.V. Calculate the dose for a patient with B.S.A. of 1.62 sq m.

2. Prescriber orders 30 mg per sq m to be added to 1 L I.V. fluid. Patient's B.S.A. is 1.58. Calculate amount to add if drug is available in a concentration of 25 mg per mL.

3. A child's B.S.A. is 0.43. Calculate the recommended dose if the usual adult dose is 150 mg.

4. A child's B.S.A. is 0.29. Calculate the recommended dose if the usual adult dose is 75 mg.

## Calculating the Rate of Delivery of I.V. Medications

In some clinical situations, drug dosages are ordered by body weight and by *rate of delivery*. In these situations, several calculations are required. You need to know the dose based on body weight, and then to determine the *hourly* dose. You must then decide on the amount of drug to add to a specific volume of intravenous fluid. Finally, you must calculate and regulate the rate of flow of the I.V. solution, either in mL per hour or drops per minute.

There are several approaches to solving these complex problems. One method is described here:

1. Calculate the required dose for the patient based on body weight.

2. Calculate the hourly dose required.

3. Determine the amount of drug to add to a specific volume of intravenous fluid. Several factors must be considered, such as stability and compatability of the drug in the I.V. fluid. These are beyond the scope of this module. If you work in a facility that provides an admixture program, this step will be completed by the pharmacy.

Example:

Mr. J. (weight: 68 kg) is ordered vidarabine monohydrate (Vira-A) 15 mg/kg/daily by constant I.V. infusion. His I.V. is infusing at 100 mL/hour.

Step 1:
Calculate the total daily dose for this patient.
$$15 \times 68 = 1\ 020 \text{ mg/day}$$

Step 2:
Calculate the hourly dose required.
$$\frac{1\ 020}{24} = 42.5 \text{ mg/hour}$$

Step 3:
Determine the amount of drug to add to a specific volume of intravenous fluid.

Let's assume that the drug can be added to a L of fluid and infused over 10 hours at the ordered rate of 100 mL/hour. What amount of drug must be added to the L?

The hourly rate is 42.5 mg, and the L will infuse in 10 hours; therefore, $42.5 \times 10 = 425$ mg should be added to the L.

Using the same clinical situation, the following examples are provided to reinforce the steps in this calculation:

---

Example:

Calculate the amount of Vira-A to be added to a 100-mL minibag and infused over 1 hour.
1. Desired dose is 1 020 mg/day
2. The hourly dose is 42.5 mg/hour
3. Add 42.5 mg to 100-mL minibag and infuse over 1 hour

---

Example:

Calculate the amount of drug to be added to 500 mL of I.V. fluid and infused at the ordered rate of 100 mL/hr.
1. Desired dose is 1 020 mg/day
2. The hourly dose is 42.5 mg/hour
3. The 500 mL bag will infuse over 5 hours; therefore, add 5 × 42.5 mg = 212.5 mg to the I.V. bag and infuse over 5 hours at 100 mL/hour

The majority of examples in this workbook have involved situations with adults and a few have involved children. The following examples are from neonatal nursing to illustrate the broad continuum of dosage calculation situations.

Example: A baby weighing 600 g is to receive gentamycin sulfate (Garamycin) 2.5 mg/kg I.V. once daily. The drug is supplied in a concentration of 10 mg/mL. Calculate the dose and amount to administer.

Dose: 2.5 mg $\times$ 0.6 kg = 1.5 mg

Amount to administer:

$$\frac{1.5 \text{ mg}}{? \text{ mL}} = \frac{10 \text{ mg}}{1 \text{ mL}}$$

10 ? = 1.5

? = 0.15 mL

Example: A baby weighing 1 500 g must receive a loading dose of theophylline elixir of 5 mg per kg orally. This is to be followed by maintenance doses of 1 mg/kg divided into 3 daily doses. Calculate the dose and the amount to administer for each order. The drug is available in a concentration of 80 mg/15 mL.

Loading dose: 5 mg $\times$ 1.5 kg = 7.5 mg

Amount to administer:

$$\frac{7.5 \text{ mg}}{? \text{ mL}} = \frac{80 \text{ mg}}{15 \text{ mL}}$$

80 ? = 112.5

? = 1.4 mL

Maintenance dose: 1 mg $\times$ 1.5 kg = 1.5 mg divided into 3 daily doses = 0.5 mg

Amount to administer for each dose:

$$\frac{0.5 \text{ mg}}{? \text{ mL}} = \frac{80 \text{ mg}}{15 \text{ mL}}$$

80 ? = 7.5

? = 0.09 mL

## Exercise 10.3

Complete the following exercise without referring to the previous text and without the aid of a calculator. Express all decimal numbers to the nearest hundredth. Correct using the answer guide.

A patient on a respirator is ordered gallamine triethiodide (Flaxedil) 1 mg per kg by continuous I.V. infusion. Calculate dosage for a patient weighing 78 kg, using each of the following available strengths:

1. 1-mL ampule containing 100 mg/mL.

2. 10-mL vial containing 20 mg/mL.

Order 1: dobutamine (Dobutrex) is ordered at 3 μg/kg/minute.

3. Using order 1, what is the dose per minute for a patient weighing 79 kg?

4. Using order 1, if the I.V. fluid contains 1 mg per mL of dobutamine, calculate the rate of infusion for a patient weighing 79 kg, using a microdrip with a drop factor of 60.

5. Using order 1, calculate the rate of infusion for the same patient, but at a dosage of 3.5 μg per kg per min.

## Accurate calculation + professional judgment = patient safety

This book has provided the learning opportunity for you to develop competence in calculating dosages in many clinical settings. The examples and exercises in each module have focused on the procedural steps involved in dosage calculations. However, administration of medications is much more than "pouring pills." This book cannot teach the principles of pharmacology and physiology needed for sound judgments and clinical safety. The reader is referred to the excellent references by Hahn et al and Johnson&Hannah listed in the bibliography.

Throughout this book, clinical situations have been presented that require professional judgment as well as calculation skills. For example, in Module 7 several calculations involved intramuscular injections. After the dosage is calculated, decisions must be made regarding the ideal site of administration and maximum volume that can be injected safely. Intravenous administration requires knowledge of many factors related to the tonicity and pH of the fluid, the administration site, and the patient. For example, in Module 9 post-test, question 10 you were asked to calculate a new rate of flow because an I.V. was behind schedule. The decision to increase the rate of flow would depend on nursing judgment of many factors.

To illustrate the importance of clinical nursing judgment, the following situation is presented. When dosages are ordered by body weight, the dose ordered may not match the available drug strength. This is shown in the following clinical situation.

For a child weighing 15.6 kg, the order is levothyroxine sodium (Synthroid) 6 $\mu$g/kg each day. The drug is available in several strengths including: orange-scored tablets, 0.025 mg each and yellow-scored tablets, 0.1 mg. The required dose per day is 15.6 $\times$ 6 $\mu$g = 93.6 $\mu$g or 0.093 6 mg. This precise dose cannot be administered from the available strengths. What are the options?

Using the orange tablets, you calculate:

$$\frac{0.093\ 6\ mg}{0.025\ mg} = 3.7\ tablets$$

The scored tablets will break evenly into halve. If you administer 3-$\frac{1}{2}$ tablets, you are giving a dose of 0.087 5 mg or 87.5 $\mu$g. This is an underdose of 6.1 $\mu$g and the child must be willing to swallow several tablets.

Using the yellow tablets, you calculate:

$$\frac{0.093\ 6\ mg}{0.1\ mg} = 0.936\ tablets$$

Since you cannot administer 0.936 tablets, you must give 1 tablet which is an overdose of 6.4 $\mu$g. However, the child must swallow only one tablet. Which option would you recommend to the prescriber?

# POST-TEST

## Instructions

1. Write the post-test without referring to any reference materials and without the aid of a calculator.

2. Correct the post-test using the answer guide.

3. If your score is 100 percent, congratulations! You have completed the final module.

4. If you don't achieve 100 percent, review the learning package in this module and rewrite the post-test. You may wish to seek further assistance through the references listed in the bibliography.

1. The drug reference book states that 25 mg per kg of Drug T. is an appropriate dose. The patient weighs 35 kg. Calculate the recommended dosage.

2. Is the following dosage within the recommended guidelines: A child weighing 15 kg is ordered Drug M. 150 mg P.O. The literature suggests 6–12 mg per kg of this drug for children.

3. An individual who weighs 70 kg is receiving 250 mg of Drug G. P.O. t.i.d. The recommended dose of this drug is 15 mg per kg per day. Is this patient receiving the recommended dose?

4. Calculate the dose to be administered:
   Ordered: 10 mg/kg P.O.
   Drug available: 200 mg tabs
   Patient weight: 60 kg

5. Calculate the dose to be administered:
   Ordered: 1 $\mu$g/kg I.V.
   Drug available: 1 mg/mL
   Patient's weight: 50 kg

6. Calculate the dose to administer:
   Order: 200 mg/m²
   Patient's B.S.A. is 0.91.
   Drug available: 150 mg/mL

7. If the usual adult dose is 75 mg, calculate the dose for a child whose B.S.A. is 0.29.

8. If the usual adult dose is 1 g, calculate the dose for a child whose B.S.A. is 0.37.

9. Order: 30 mg/kg P.O. daily in 3 divided doses. Patient weighs 65 kg. Calculate each dose.

10. Order: 10 mg/kg I.V. q.6h. Patient weighs 55 kg. Calculate each dose to add to the I.V. if available strength is 1 g/mL.

Order 1: 2 $\mu$g/kg/minute I.V.

11. For order 1, calculate dosage required for a patient weighing 63 kg.

12. For order 1, if the I.V. solution contains 1 mg per mL, calculate the rate of flow to deliver the correct dose for a patient weighing 60 kg. Administration set delivers 60 drops per mL.

13.  An intravenous is infusing at 15 drops per minute (drop factor is 60). The concentration of drug is 80 mg in 100 mL I.V. fluid. How much drug is $\mu$g is infusing each minute?

14.  If the usual adult dose is 10 mg, calculate the dose for a child with a B.S.A. of 0.2 sq m. The drug is available in 5 mg per mL.

15.  Calculate the dose for a patient with a B.S.A. of 1.12. Order is for 500 mg per sq m, and the drug is available in 250 mg per mL.

YOUR SCORE: _____ %

100%     YES—you have reached the end of this series of modules. Bravo!
         NO—review this module

**Note:** if you had any errors on the post-test, analyze your areas of weakness here before reviewing the appropriate section of the module.

# Answer Guide

## Module 1

### Pre-test

1. 1 223
2. 2 517
3. 814
4. 594
5. 899
6. 501
7. 475
8. 1 354
9. 311
10. 53
11. 789
12. 102
13. 2 608
14. 5 440
15. 51 684
16. 8 385
17. 890 415
18. 2 189 094
19. 18
20. 2
21. 5
22. 8
23. 5
24. 8
25. 13
26. 6
27. 30
28. 7
29. $20.00
30. $10.00

### Exercise 1.1

1. 1 627
2. 163 600
3. 8 884
4. 20 001
5. 11 965
6. 908 278

### Exercise 1.2

1. 89
2. 403
3. 89
4. 26
5. 203 529
6. 11 199

### Exercise 1.3

1. 156
2. 353 256
3. 3 333
4. 3 550 635
5. 2 010 300
6. 25 515

### Exercise 1.4

1. 2
2. 31
3. 4
4. 13
5. 984
6. 125

### Exercise 1.5

1. 2
2. 22
3. 1
4. 5 474
5. 9 090
6. 67 000
7. 203
8. 8 118
9. 30 527
10. 200

## Exercise 1.6

1. $6.50
2. $262.00
3. $3.00
4. 3
5. 16 sticks of licorice and forty cents change

## Post-test

1. 26 707
2. 59 231
3. 523
4. 403 018
5. 801
6. 1 134
7. 5 131
8. 31
9. 63
10. 229
11. 191
12. 902
13. 2 047
14. 210 105
15. 30 906
16. 1 000
17. 10 100
18. 4 653
19. 3
20. 101
21. 201
22. 9
23. 40
24. 40
25. 13 822
26. $12.50
27. 5
28. $2.25
29. 11 days
30. $130.15

## Module 2

### Pre-test

1. $3 \frac{13}{20}$
2. $1 \frac{7}{30}$
3. $2 \frac{3}{4}$
4. $7 \frac{7}{24}$
5. $\frac{47}{72}$
6. $\frac{13}{20}$
7. $2 \frac{9}{16}$
8. $2 \frac{15}{16}$
9. $\frac{1}{2}$
10. $14 \frac{5}{8}$
11. $4 \frac{4}{5}$
12. $31 \frac{1}{2}$
13. $\frac{8}{9}$
14. 3
15. $101 \frac{1}{3}$
16. $\frac{3}{16}$
17. $3 \frac{3}{5}$
18. $7 \frac{6}{11}$
19. $8 \frac{1}{6}$
20. $3 \frac{25}{34}$
21. 4
22. 30
23. 40
24. 24
25. $\frac{7}{8}$
26. $\frac{1}{4}$
27. $\frac{2}{3}$

28. $\frac{3}{7}$
29. Proper fraction
30. Improper fraction
31. Mixed number
32. Proper fraction
33. $\frac{3}{6}$
34. $\frac{9}{60}$
35. $\frac{21}{27}$
36. $\frac{49}{70}$
37. 9
38. $\frac{4}{8}$ or $\frac{1}{2}$
39. 32
40. $\frac{1}{8}$

## Exercise 2.1

1. Proper
2. Proper
3. Mixed number
4. Improper
5. Proper
6. Mixed number
7. $\frac{1}{3}$
8. $\frac{1}{2}$
9. $\frac{1}{2}$
10. $\frac{5}{8}$
11. Cannot be reduced
12. $\frac{1}{2}$
13. Cannot be reduced
14. Cannot be reduced
15. No
16. Yes
17. Yes
18. Yes
19. $\frac{9}{21}$
20. $\frac{16}{20}$
21. $\frac{10}{15}$
22. $\frac{6}{30}$

## Exercise 2.2

1. $\frac{49}{8}$
2. $\frac{11}{2}$
3. $\frac{14}{4}$
4. $\frac{79}{10}$
5. $\frac{38}{3}$
6. $4\frac{7}{8}$

7. $2\frac{3}{4}$
8. 3
9. $3\frac{1}{3}$
10. $10\frac{5}{12}$

## Exercise 2.3

1. $1\frac{11}{21}$
2. $\frac{19}{30}$
3. $1\frac{17}{24}$
4. $\frac{31}{32}$
5. $1\frac{5}{8}$
6. $\frac{13}{14}$
7. $1\frac{1}{30}$
8. $\frac{7}{9}$
9. $\frac{19}{20}$
10. $\frac{15}{16}$

## Exercise 2.4

1. $\frac{5}{28}$
2. $\frac{19}{30}$
3. $\frac{13}{24}$
4. $\frac{11}{20}$
5. $\frac{2}{9}$
6. $\frac{1}{40}$
7. $\frac{1}{12}$
8. $\frac{4}{15}$
9. $\frac{17}{144}$
10. $\frac{13}{24}$

## Exercise 2.5

1. $1\frac{13}{14}$
2. $2\frac{2}{5}$
3. $7\frac{1}{12}$
4. $3\frac{17}{24}$
5. $4\frac{2}{9}$
6. $1\frac{1}{12}$
7. $1\frac{2}{9}$
8. $2\frac{1}{10}$
9. $2\frac{1}{4}$
10. $\frac{11}{28}$

# Exercise 2.6

1. $\frac{10}{21}$
2. 1
3. $\frac{1}{16}$
4. $\frac{3}{16}$
5. 75
6. $5\frac{5}{6}$
7. $2\frac{2}{3}$
8. $2\frac{11}{12}$
9. $1\frac{1}{4}$
10. $5\frac{1}{8}$

# Exercise 2.7

1. $1\frac{1}{14}$
2. 9
3. $4\frac{1}{4}$
4. $1\frac{1}{48}$
5. $\frac{3}{400}$
6. $1\frac{1}{4}$
7. 22
8. 12
9. $\frac{2}{3}$
10. 250

# Exercise 2.8

1. $\frac{23}{40}$
2. 40 students (or $\frac{8}{9}$)
3. No: should be $1\frac{1}{5}$
4. No: should be $\frac{1}{4}$
5. 12 ounces

# Post-test

1. $\frac{25}{28}$
2. $1\frac{21}{40}$
3. $14\frac{7}{12}$

4. $\frac{43}{60}$
5. $\frac{17}{36}$
6. $2\frac{1}{3}$
7. $20\frac{1}{16}$
8. $\frac{5}{24}$
9. $\frac{2}{21}$
10. $\frac{3}{5}$
11. $7\frac{2}{3}$
12. 3
13. $\frac{3}{4}$
14. $9\frac{3}{4}$
15. $\frac{5}{12}$
16. $\frac{50}{63}$
17. $4\frac{1}{5}$
18. $4\frac{2}{9}$
19. $12\frac{5}{7}$
20. $16\frac{11}{12}$
21. 72
22. 48
23. 72
24. 42
25. $\frac{4}{9}$
26. $\frac{5}{9}$
27. $\frac{5}{6}$
28. 3
29. $\frac{8}{9}$
30. $\frac{14}{11}$
31. $1\frac{2}{3}$
32. $\frac{35}{49}$
33. $\frac{28}{70}$
34. $\frac{60}{108}$
35. $\frac{30}{200}$
36. $\frac{32}{44}$
37. 17
38. 80
39. 20 minutes
40. $\frac{1}{5}$

# Module 3

## Pre-test

1. 0.25

2. 1
3. 0.12
4. 3.4
5. 7.1

6. 1.2
7. 9.2
8. 12.46
9. 6.10 (or 6.1)
10. 34 .00 (or 34)
11. 4.91
12. 2.547
13. 126.034 2
14. 6.27
15. 3.732
16. 6.3
17. 3.3
18. 4.52
19. 0.05
20. 8
21. 80
22. 800
23. 0.001
24. 0.5
25. 66.66 (repeating)
26. 2.2233 (repeating)
27. 44.5
28. 0.8
29. 0.5
30. 0.3
31. 0.8
32. $\frac{3}{5}$ or $\frac{6}{10}$
33. $\frac{57}{100}$
34. $1\frac{1}{4}$
35. $\frac{1}{100}$
36. 0.000 1   0.01   0.1   1.001   1.101
37. $1.20
38. $11.70
39. $95.40
40. $11.37

## Exercise 3.1

1. correct
2. 1.7
3. correct
4. 0.35
5. 1.4
6. 1.9
7. 1
8. 1.1
9. 6.33
10. 2.09
11. 0.95
12. 7.67
13. 1.055   1.105   1.15   1.515
14. 50.6   5.06   0.506

## Exercise 3.2

1. 6.44
2. 14.373
3. 11.21
4. 1.76
5. 2.046 1
6. 40 074.821

## Exercise 3.3

1. 4.064
2. 3.822
3. 3.426 52
4. 58.143 06
5. 4.3
6. 879.4
7. 0.5
8. 1 000 250

## Exercise 3.4

1. $\frac{1}{8}$
2. $2\frac{1}{2}$
3. $\frac{4}{5}$
4. $\frac{3}{4}$
5. $1\frac{3}{4}$
6. 0.75
7. 0.05
8. 3.83
9. 0.33 (repeating)
10. 1.25

## Exercise 3.5

1. 150%
2. 37%
3. 17%
4. 94%
5. 6.66% (repeating)
6. 83.33% (repeating)
7. 72.72% (repeating)
8. 79%
9. 0.77
10. 0.01
11. 0.29
12. 0.82

## Post-test

1. 4.15
2. 1.77
3. 1.26
4. 1.32
5. 2.33
6. 1.89
7. 1.19
8. 2.42
9. 10.63
10. 0.3
11. 4.25
12. 101
13. 180
14. 0.13
15. 2
16. 3
17. 4.2
18. 1.8
19. 1.3
20. 2.3
21. 1.89
22. 1.97
23. 10.64
24. 0.36
25. 0.67
26. 1.25
27. 0.88
28. 2.5
29. $\frac{19}{25}$
30. $1\frac{3}{10}$
31. $\frac{13}{100}$
32. $\frac{1}{20}$
33. 0.5
34. 1.2
35. 1.01
36. 1.901, 1.991, 10.01, 10.1
37. $451.08
38. $386.77
39. $3.92
40. $527.14

## Module 4

### Pre-test

1. 45
2. 12
3. 25
4. 4
5. 4
6. 3
7. $\frac{1}{100}$
8. 0.01
9. 1%
10. $\frac{1}{5}$
11. 0.2
12. 20%
13. $\frac{1}{250}$
14. 0.004
15. 0.4%
16. 7:5
17. 5:1
18. 17:3
19. A relationship that exists between two quantities.
20. An equation between two equal ratios.

### Exercise 4.1

1. 1:9
2. 9:10
3. 325 units/tablet: or 325:1
4. 25 units/teaspoon or 25:1
5. 1:4

### Exercise 4.2

1. 8
2. 25
3. 21
4. 2
5. 1.5
6. 1.33
7. 0.37
8. 0.5
9. 0.25
10. 1

### Exercise 4.3

1. $\frac{1}{25}$
2. 0.04
3. 4%

4. $\frac{1}{10}$
5. 0.1
6. 10%
7. $\frac{7}{9}$
8. 0.8
9. 77.8%
10. $\frac{25}{2}$
11. 12.5
12. 1 250%
13. $\frac{50}{1}$
14. 50
15. 5 000%
16. $\frac{10}{1}$
17. 10
18. 1 000%
19. 3:4
20. 333:1 000
21. 1:2
22. 1:200

## Post-test

1. 9
2. 8

3. 10
4. 23:39
5. 3:17
6. A relationship that exists between two quantities.
7. An equation between two equal ratios.
8. 7
9. 10 units/teaspoon
10. No: the two ratios are not equal. Validate by multiplication:

$$\frac{6}{32} = ? \frac{24}{100}$$

$6 \times 100 = 600$
$32 \times 24 = 768$

11. $\frac{0.9}{100}$ or 9:1 000
12. $\frac{1}{1}$
13. 1
14. 100%
15. $\frac{2}{3}$
16. 0.7
17. 66.7%
18. $\frac{1}{1\ 000}$
19. 0.001
20. 0.1%

# Module 5

## Pre-test

1. metre, m
2. kilogram, kg
3. mole, mol
4. 0.1
5. 0.01
6. 0.001
7. 0.000 000 001
8. 0.000 001
9. 1 000
10. 1 000 mg
11. 1 000 mL
12. 0.01 g
13. 1 000 g
14. 0.001 g
15. 0.25 L
16. 0.04 kg

17. 0.2 g
18. 300 mg
19. 100 cm
20. 2.5 m
21. 600 mg
22. 60 mL
23. 5 mL
24. 6.6 lb
25. 182.88 cm

## Exercise 5.1

1. k
2. d
3. c
4. m
5. $\mu$

6. 1 000
7. 0.000 000 001
8. 0.000 000 000 001
9. 0.001
10. 0.000 001
11. 0.01
12. kilo, hecto, deci, centi, milli, micro, nano, pico

## Exercise 5.2

1. m
2. 10 kg
3. 0.5 mL
4. L
5. 1 000 mL
6. 51 517
7. true

## Exercise 5.3

1. 1 000
2. 1 000
3. 100
4. 1
5. 1 000 000
6. 0.25
7. 500
8. 200
9. 1 000
10. 0.001
11. 0.3
12. 0.8
13. 1.5
14. 750
15. 2.5

## Exercise 5.4

1. 79.54
2. 79.5
3. 80
4. 55
5. 4 feet 7 inches
6. 5
7. 30

## Post-test

1. 2 000
2. 0.25
3. 2
4. 6 000
5. 7 000
6. 5
7. 0.001 25
8. 3
9. 2 500
10. 500
11. 1.456
12. 0.000 5
13. 1 000
14. 170
15. 1.79
16. 500
17. 0.25
18. 1 340
19. 10 000 000
20. 79 000 000
21. 0.01
22. 0.001
23. 0.000 001
24. 1 000
25. 0.1

# Module 6

## Pre-test

1. Morphine sulfate 10 to 15 mg intramuscular every four hours as necessary
2. Insulin 6 units subcutaneous immediately
3. Metoclopramide 10 mg by mouth, 1 hour before meals, three times a day
4. Aluminum hydroxide 30 mL by mouth, 1 hour after meals, three times a day
5. Flurazepam hydrochloride 15 mg by mouth at bedtime
6. A = tablet; B = solution (or liquid)
7. A = 5 mg per tablet; B = 10 mg per mL
8. Dosage
9. Route
10. False: contains slighly more than 1 mL to allow extra fluid to fill needle.
11. E
12. G
13. F
14. C
15. H
16. I
17. B
18. A
19. D
20. J

## Exercise 6.1

1. Meperidine 50 to 75 mg intramuscular every three to four hours as necessary
2. Acetaminophen 650 mg by mouth every four hours
3. Codeine 60 mg by mouth immediately and every four hours
4. Penicillin 500 000 units intravenous four times a day
5. Phenobarbital elixir 100 mg at bedtime
6. Patient

7. Drug
8. Dosage or dose
9. Route
10. Frequency or time of administration

## Exercise 6.2

1. Enteric-coated tablets
2. 150 mg per tablet
3. 100 tablets
4. 15 000 mg or 15 grams
5. Solution
6. 20 mg per mL (100 mg per 5 mL)
7. 100 mL
8. 2 000 mg or 2 grams
9. Solution
10. 1 000 $\mu$g per mL (or 1 mg/mL)
11. 10 mL
12. 10 000 mcg or 10 mg

## Post-test

Part One: crossword

| Across | Down |
|--------|------|
| 1. PRN | 1. PO |
| 3. Q4H | 2. UNG |
| 5. STAT | 3. QID |
| 8. PC | 4. HS |
| 10. BID | 6. TID |
| 12. AC | 7. TAB |
| 13. QS | 9. CAPS |
| | 11. IM |
| | 13. QH |

Part Two:

a. Solution
b. 20 mL
c. 5 mEq (milliequivalents) per mL
d. 100 mEq (milliequivalents)

## Module 7

### Pre-test

1.  0.8 mL
2.  3 tabs (0.015 g = 15 mg)
3.  2 tabs
4.  0.4 mL
5.  2 tabs (1 g = 1 000 mg)
6.  1.5 tabs
7.  2 tabs
8.  $\frac{1}{2}$ tab
9.  3 tabs
10. 0.22 mL
11. 0.12 mL
12. 0.34 mL
13. 0.7 mL
14. $\frac{1}{2}$ tab (0.5 tab)
15. 1.5 mL
16. 168 caps
17. 0.75 mL
18. Error: 0.5 mL must include 0 before decimal
19. Error: 1 mL not ampule. Ampules contain extra volume to allow for loss. The ampule may contain 1.1 mL and this represents a dosage error of 10%.
20. Error: 0.5 mL
21. Correct
22. No: volume should be 4.3 mL
23. 0.6 mL
24. Administer all the solution: it will be slightly greater than 1 mL because of volume of powder.
25. 1 g/mL

### Exercise 7.1

1.  2 tabs
2.  3 tabs (1.5 g = 1 500 mg)
3.  2 tabs (0.2 g = 200 mg)
3.  1 $\frac{1}{2}$ tabs (1.5 tabs)
5.  2 tabs
6.  Either: 6 of the 5 mg tablets or 1 of the 20 mg tabs and 2 of the 5 mg tabs
7.  $\frac{1}{2}$ tab (0.5 tab)
8.  2 tabs
9.  $\frac{1}{2}$ tab (0.5 tab)
10. 2 caps (0.5 g = 500 mg)

### Exercise 7.2

1.  0.75 mL
2.  75 mg
3.  15 mL
4.  1.5 mL
5.  2 mL
6.  ⎫
7.  ⎪
8.  ⎬  see next page
9.  ⎪
10. ⎭

6.

7.

8.

9.

10.

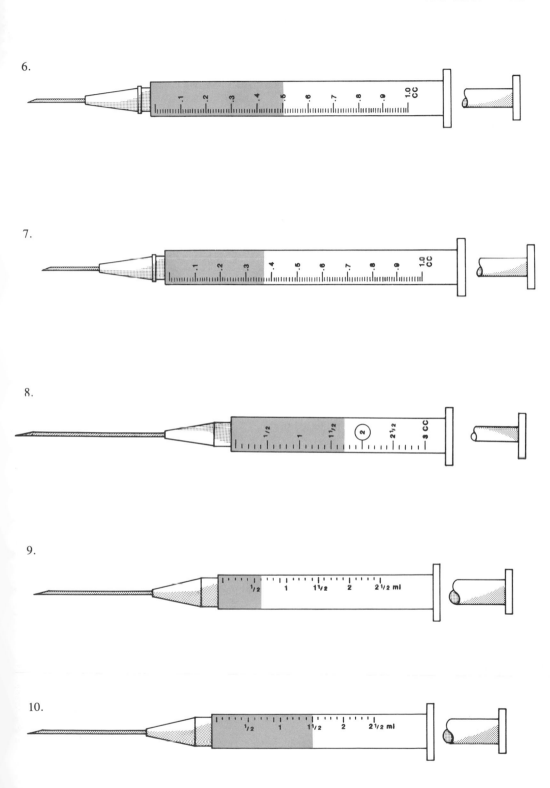

## Exercise 7.3

1. 9.3 mL
2. 1.33 mL (1 mL = 750 000 units)
3. 3.75 mL
4. 2 mL
5. 1.25 mL
6. 750 000 units
7. 600 000 units
8. 1 050 000 units
9. 10 mL
10. 10 doses

## Exercise 7.4

1. 0.75 mL
2. 3 tabs
3. 2 tabs
4. 0.34 mL
5. 2 tabs
6. 2 mL
7. 3 tabs
8. 1.5 mL
9. 1.5 tabs
10. 0.5 mL
11. 0.5 tab
12. 0.6 mL
13. 2 tabs
14. 8 tabs
15. 56 tabs
16. Give 1 tab not 1 mg
17. No: give 1 mL not 1 ampule: ampule is not a measurement
18. No: give 1 mL: 50 is NOT REASONABLE!
19. No: give 2 tablets $\frac{1}{2}$ hour AFTER meals
20. Correct

## Post-test

**Note:** mark your answers as correct only if you have included the correct units as well as the correct numerical answer.

1. 3 tabs (0.3 g = 300 mg)
2. 1.5 tabs (or $1\frac{1}{2}$ tabs)
3. 1.3 mL
4. 2 tabs
5. 2 mL
6. 2 tabs (0.65 g = 650 mg)
7. 0.25 mL
8. 2 tabs
9. a. 2.5 mL for 1 000 units/mL strength
   b. 0.25 mL for 10 000 unit/mL strength
10. 0.35 mL
11. 0.15 mL
12. 0.5 mL
13. 7 tabs
14. 2 tabs (1 000 mg = 1 g)
15. 1 000 000 units mL
16. 0.5 mL
17. 20 dosages (each 500 000 units)
18. 1 mL
19. 0.67 mL
20. 1.67 mL
21. Yes, 0.3 mL is correct
22. 1.5 tabs
23. 4.17 mL
24. 1.5 mL
25. 3.75 mg daily

# Module 8

## Pre-test

1. A *solute* is the substance that is dissolved in a solvent.
2. A *solution* is a homogeneous mixture which contains one or more dissolved substances in a liquid.
3. A *solvent* is the liquid in which another substance is dissolved.
4. The *strength* or *concentration* of a solution is determined by the amount of *solute* dissolved in a given amount of solvent.
5. 100
6. 5, 100
7. mL
8. 9:1 000
9. b

10. b
11. 1:20
12. 3:1 000
13. 33:1 000
14. 3:5
15. 1:10
16. 9:1 000
17. 5%
18. 500%
19. 0.1%
20. 25%
21. 0.01%
22. 9 g of salt
23. 25 g of dextrose
24. 1 mg of epincphrinc

| | Ratio | Percent |
|---|---|---|
| 25. | 1:500 | 0.2% |
| 26. | 1:60 | 1.66% (repeating) |
| 27. | 1:200 | 0.5% |
| 28. | 1:50 | 2% |
| 29. | 1:2 | 50% |
| 30. | 1.1 000 | 0.1% |

## Exercise 8.1

1. solution
2. solute
3. solvent
4. penicillin G potassium
5. water
6. true
7. b
8. a

## Exercise 8.2

1. g
2. mL
3. mL
4. mL
5. weight per volume (w/v) solution
6. volume per volume (v/v) solution

## Exercise 8.3

1. A percent strength describes how many parts of solute (drug) are contained in 100 parts of solution.

2. A ratio describes the number of parts of solute to the number of parts of solution.
3. 1:5
4. 15 in 100

## Exercise 8.4

1. 4%
2. 0.1%
3. 0.01%
4. 7.5%
5. 100%
6. 10:100 or 1:10
7. 45:10 000 or 9:2 000
8. 25:100 or 1:4
9. 33:1 000
10. 5:100 or 1:20

## Exercise 8.5

1. Amount of pure drug = ?
   strength = 1:1 000 or $\frac{1}{1\ 000}$
   volume = 0.1 mL

   Weight/volume solution: expressing grams of drug per mL
   Substitute values into formula #1 and calculate:

   $? = \frac{1}{1\ 000} \times 0.1$
   ? = 0.0001 grams

   Express in milligrams
   = 0.0001 × 1 000 = 0.1 mg

   The patient will receive 0.1 mg of epinephrine.

2. Amount of pure drug = 10μg
   expressed as grams = 0.00001 grams
   strength = 1:1 000 or $\frac{1}{1\ 000}$
   volume = ?

   Calculation:

   $0.00001 = \frac{1}{1\ 000} \times$ ?
   ? = 0.01 mL

   to give a dose of 10 μg, administer 0.01 mL of 1:1 000 epinephrine.

3. ?(1) is the ordered dose.
   $?(1) = \frac{1}{1\ 000} \times 0.5$
   ?(1) = 0.0005 grams or 0.5 mg

?(2) is the administered dose.

$$?(2) = \frac{1}{10\ 000} \times 0.5$$
$$?(2) = 0.00005 \text{ grams or } 0.05 \text{ mg}$$

The dosage error $= ?(2) - ?(1)$
$0.05 - 0.5$ mg $= -0.45$ mg
The patient was underdosed by 0.45 mg, or a tenfold dosage error occurred.

4. Amount of drug $= ?$
   Strength $= 5\%$ or $\frac{5}{100}$
   Volume $= 500$ mL
   Weight per volume solution (g to mL)

   $$? = \frac{5g}{100\ mL} \times 500 \text{ mL}$$
   $$? = 25$$

   There are 25 g of dextrose in 500 mL of a 5% solution.

5. Amount of drug (saline) $= ?$
   Strength $= 0.9\%$ or $\frac{9}{1\ 000}$
   Volume $= 1$ litre or $1\ 000$ mL
   Weight per volume solution (g to mL)

   $$? = \frac{9}{1\ 000} \times 1\ 000$$
   $$? = 9 \text{ g of salt are needed}$$

## Exercise 8.6

1. Amount of drug = strength × volume
   (g or mL)         (% or ratio  (mL)
                      expressed as
                      a fraction)

   $50 = ? \%$ or $\frac{?}{100} \times 1\ 000$
   $? = 5$
   Answer $= 5\%$ solution

2. $0.001 \text{ g} = \frac{?}{100} \times 1$
   $? = 0.001 \times 100$
   $? = 0.1$
   Expressed as a ratio strength:
   0.1:100 or 1:1 000
   Ratios should be expressed in whole numbers!

3. $0.25 \text{ g} = \frac{?}{100} \times 1$
   $? = 0.25 \times 100$
   $? = 25$
   Answer: 25% solution

4. Answer: c

## Post-test

1. 1:20
2. 3:1 000
3. 33:1 000
4. 3:5
5. 1:10
6. 9:1 000
7. 5%
8. 500%
9. 0.1%
10. 25%
11. 0.01%
12. 9 g of salt
13. 25 g of dextrose
14. 1 mg of epinephrine

| | Ratio | Percent |
|---|---|---|
| 15. | 1:1 000 | 0.1% |
| 16. | 1:1 000 | 0.1% |
| 17. | 1:20 | 5% |
| 18. | 1:4 | 25% |
| 19. | 1:2 | 50% |
| 20. | 3:200 | 1.5% |

21. A *solute* is the substance dissolved in a solvent.
22. A *solution* is a homogeneous mixture that contains one or more dissolved substances in a liquid.
23. A *solvent* is the liquid in which another substance is dissolved.
24. The *strength* or *concentration* of a solution is determined by the amount of *solute* dissolved in a given amount of solvent.
25. 100
26. g (weight), mL (volume)
27. mL
28. Ratio
29. b
30. b

# Module 9

## Pre-test

1. 2 mL/min approximately
2. 21 drops/min approximately
3. 17 hours
4. 83 mL/hour
5. Approximately 83 drops/min
6. 25 drops/min
7. 83 mL/hour
8. Approximately 83 drops/min
9. 10 drops/min
10. 562.5 mL
11. 50 drops/minute
12. No: should be 17 drops/min (approximately)
13. 8 hours
14. 42 drops/min
15. 2 hours

## Exercise 9.1

1. 83 drops/min (approximately)
2. 20 hours
3. 21 drops (approximately)
4. 125 drops/min
5. 100 mL/hour
6. 3 630 mL
7. 151 h
8. 25 drops/min
9. 167 drops/min
10. 42 drops/min

## Post-test

1. 125 drops/min
2. Approximately 21 drops/min
3. Volume required is 100 L of I.V. fluid dilute 100 mg drug in 100 mL I.V. fluid: infuse over 2 hours = 50 mL and therefore 50 mg/hour
4. 50 drops/min
5. 25 mg of aminophylline
6. 10 hours: 500 mg drop added to 500 mL of I.V. fluid to provide a concentration of 1 mg/mL: infuse at 50 mg (and therefore 50 mL) per hour.
7. 50 mL of I.V. fluid: add 250 mg of drug to 50 mL of I.V. fluid to provide a concentration of 5 mg/mL
8. 100 drops/min
9. 375 mL should have been absorbed in 3 hours. The I.V. is behind 75 mL.
10. New rate is 23 drops/min
11. 28 drops/min
12. 60 minutes or 1 hour
13. 1200 hours
14. 1 500 mL
15. 480 mL

# Module 10

## Pre-test

1. 1 tablet
2. 0.1 mL
3. 500 mg
4. 2 tablets
5. 0.9 g
6. 6.94 mg
7. 144.51 mg
8. 24.86 mg
9. Approximately 16 drops/min
10. 130 µg/min
11. 800 µg/mL
12. Approximately 10 drops/min
13. 4 µg/mL
14. 6.5 mg
15. 200 µg or 0.2 mg/min

## Exercise 10.1

1. 3.4 mL
2. 0.92 mL
3. 0.27 mL
4. No: 0.34 mg is within the recommended amount
5. 250 mg

## Exercise 10.2

1. 972 mg
2. 1.89 mL
3. 37.28 mg
4. 12.57 mg

## Exercise 10.3

1. 0.78 mL
2. 3.9 mL
3. 237 $\mu$g/min
4. 14 drops/min
5. 16.59 or 17 drops/min

## Post-test

1. 875 mg
2. Yes: recommended dosages ranges from 90–180
3. No: it is lower than recommended dosage of 1 050 daily
4. 3 tabs
5. 0.05 mL
6. 1.21 mL
7. 12.57 mg
8. 0.213 g or 213.87 mg
9. 650 mg
10. 0.55 mL
11. 126 $\mu$g/min
12. 7 drops/min
13. 200 $\mu$g/min
14. 0.23 mL
15. 2.24 mL

# APPENDIX

## Calculating Pediatric Dosages on Body Mass or Age

---

**Clark's Rule**

$$\text{Child's dose} = \frac{\text{Mass of child}}{150 \text{ lb or } 68 \text{ kg}} \times \text{Adult dose}$$

---

**Fried's Rule (Birth–12 months)**

$$\text{Infant's dose} = \frac{\text{Age (in months)}}{150} \times \text{Adult dose}$$

---

**Young's Rule (1–12 years)**

$$\text{Child's dose} = \frac{\text{Age (in yr)}}{\text{Age (in yr)} + 12} \times \text{Adult dose}$$

# Bibliography

Bayt PT. Administering Medications: a Competency-based Program for Health Oc-
    cupations. Indianapolis: Bobb-Merrill Educational Publishing, 1982.
Cordon MJ. Clinical Calculations for Nurses. Englewood Cliffs: Prentice-Hall, 1984.
Glenn J, McCaugherty D. SI units for nurses. New York: Harper&Row, Publishers,
    1981.
Hahn A, Oestrich S, Barkin R. Mosby's Pharmacology in Nursing. St. Louis: C.V.
    Mosby Company, 1986; 16th ed.
Howry L, Bindler R. Pediatric Medications. Toronto: J.B. Lippincott, 1981.
Johnson G, Hannah K. Pharmacology and the Nursing Process. Philadelphia: W.
    B. Saunders, 1986; 2nd ed.
Miller M. Mathematics for Nurses: with Clinical Applications. Monterey:
    Brooks/Cole Publishing Company, 1981.
Richardson L Jr, Richardson J. Mathematics of Drugs and Solutions with Clinical
    Application. New York: McGraw-Hill Company, 1980; 2nd ed.
Roach, AC. Standardized Infusion Concentrations of Cardiovascular Drugs. *Criti-
    cal Care Nurse*, 3(2), p. 98.
Sackheim G, Robins L. Programmed Mathematics for Nurses. Toronto: Collier-
    Macmillan Canada, Inc, 1983; 5th ed.
The S.I. Manual in Health Care. Toronto: Government of Ontario, 1982; 2nd ed.